Cambridge Elements ☰

Elements in Religion in Late Antiquity
edited by
Andrew S. Jacobs
Harvard Divinity School

THEORY, HISTORY, AND THE STUDY OF RELIGION IN LATE ANTIQUITY

Speculative Worlds

Maia Kotrosits
University of Waterloo

CAMBRIDGE
UNIVERSITY PRESS

Shaftesbury Road, Cambridge CB2 8EA, United Kingdom

One Liberty Plaza, 20th Floor, New York, NY 10006, USA

477 Williamstown Road, Port Melbourne, VIC 3207, Australia

314–321, 3rd Floor, Plot 3, Splendor Forum, Jasola District Centre,
New Delhi – 110025, India

103 Penang Road, #05–06/07, Visioncrest Commercial, Singapore 238467

Cambridge University Press is part of Cambridge University Press & Assessment,
a department of the University of Cambridge.

We share the University's mission to contribute to society through the pursuit of
education, learning and research at the highest international levels of excellence.

www.cambridge.org
Information on this title: www.cambridge.org/9781009012003

DOI: 10.1017/9781009025560

First published 2023

A catalogue record for this publication is available from the British Library.

ISBN 978-1-009-01200-3 Paperback
ISSN 2633-8602 (online)
ISSN 2633-8599 (print)

Theory, History, and the Study of Religion in Late Antiquity

Speculative Worlds

Elements in Religion in Late Antiquity

DOI: 10.1017/9781009025560
First published online: January 2023

Maia Kotrosits
University of Waterloo

Author for correspondence: Maia Kotrosits, maiakotrosits@gmail.com

Abstract: Theory is not a set of texts, it is a style of approach. It is to engage in the act of speculation: gestures of abstraction that reimagine and dramatize the crises of living. This Element is both a primer for understanding some of the more predominant strands of critical theory in the study of religion in late antiquity, and a history of speculative leaps in the field. It is a history of dilemmas that the field has tried to work out again and again – questions about subjectivity, the body, agency, violence, and power. This Element additionally presses us on the ethical stakes of our uses of theory and asks how the field's interests in theory help us understand what is going on, half-spoken, in the disciplinary unconscious.

Keywords: religion, late antiquity, theory, gender, postcolonial studies

ISBNs: 9781009012003 (PB), 9781009025560 (OC)
ISSNs: 2633-8602 (online), 2633-8599 (print)

Contents

Introduction

> I can only speak for myself. But what I write and how I write is done in order to save my own life. And I mean that literally.
>
> Barbara Christian, *"The Race for Theory"*

Let's start with this: theory is not a set of texts, it is a style of approach. Despite what it seems, to "do theory" is not to master a particular set of philosophical or critical ideas. Or at least it should not be. It is certainly not to "apply" them, which suggests the ideas are inanimate or inert. It is something more: it is to "play with possibility" as Barbara Christian puts it, to do urgent retelling of the conditions of the world.[1] Such work far exceeds any modern canons or formulaic hermeneutical strategies. It is to get a little lost in the act of speculation.[2]

I start here with Barbara Christian, who back in 1987 launched an important critique of the narrow aperture – and striking whiteness – of "theory" after the 1960s and 1970s, in order to follow her in the task of beginning to loosen our attachments to this canon and the apparent demand that we instrumentalize it, as opposed to, say, taking its invitation to speculate. I start with Barbara Christian, and I will end with her, to return us to the necessity, sometimes dire, of this retelling and conscious play that is so often the engine for our collective dives into theory (typically understood).[3]

This Element, then, will only partially be a pedagogical rendition of when and how the relatively small canon of philosophical texts over-associated with theory has appeared in the study of religion in late antiquity.[4] I begin but do not end there. In starting with "theory" traditionally understood, I hope to stretch us toward readings outside of this canon, toward practices other than "use" and

---

[1] Barbara Christian, "The race for theory," *Cultural Critique*, 6 (1987), 51–63.

[2] Speculation, while a synonym for theory, more directly implicates imagination, fantasy, and play. It points to theory as process, rather than as specialized jargon, schematics, or grand epistemologies. So my choice of the word "speculation" here comes from a desire to foreground creativity while also being clear about its gravity and necessity.

[3] There is much more to Christian's piece than what I have recounted thus far, some of which I will discuss at the Conclusion of this Element. It is important to note here, though, that Christian is writing about Black art and literature as theorizing, as world-making, and her essay and her writing at large have been central to Black feminism. So there is an inevitable disjoint in bringing her critique and call into the context of a predominantly white field like ancient history. I believe understanding and taking seriously her critique and call, however, is crucial to crafting a more ethical and, because more ethical, more vital field of thought.

[4] There have already been very full accounts and explanations of theory in or overlapping with the field of late antiquity studies. The two main examples, both elegant and programmatic, are Elizabeth A. Clark, *History, Theory, Text: Historians and the Linguistic Turn* (Harvard University Press, 2004) and Michal Beth Dinkler, *Literary Theory and the New Testament* (Yale University Press, 2019). More extensive and wide-ranging, written by a collection of authors, and not unlike the Elements series, is Brill's Research Perspectives in Biblical Interpretation series. The fact that this work has already been done so well allows me to depart a bit from instructional and cartographical modes.

"application" of theory – to put our current relationship to theory/particular theories back into the context of the crises of living they attempt to resolve. I expect that moving toward these other readings and practices will sometimes be difficult and far from obvious.

To initiate this movement, I have written this Element as a history of speculative leaps in the field, often as they appear with or near what we designate as theory. It is a history of dilemmas that the field has tried to work out again and again, for which the field tried to find new (and then old, and then new) language and concepts. It is a history of intractability, impasses, and irresolution for historical, experiential, and existential questions, because often it is "theory" that is brought in to resolve or mediate these large-scale questions – ones that animate our work because they animate our lives. This Element also contains my own speculations on why we as a field are here now, and about what is going on, half-spoken, in the disciplinary unconscious.

I do not aim for comprehensiveness, either bibliographic or otherwise (over-rated if not impossible). The goal is less to survey the breadth of material engaging theory in the study of religion in late antiquity than it is to offer a synthesis and primer for how to understand and connect at least the most predominant strands and themes associated with "theory" in the field.[5] These are strands and themes that generally fall under the heading of contemporary critical theory and cultural studies.[6]

This Element is structured in three sections, each beginning with a short portrait of a pivotal and early figure in the study of religion in late antiquity: Elizabeth Clark, Peter Brown, and Henri-Irénée Marrou. They are addressed in that order. I approach each scholar through dilemmas that centrally preoccupied them, and I follow the trail of those dilemmas as they lived on in the field, either through explicit struggle or subtle and underground fixations and attachments. I choose these three scholars to frame the sections not just for their influence or status as beloved figures, but because of the way these "early" figures in the field crystallize specific ongoing tensions between living history and writing history, tensions that demanded gestures of abstraction and imagination to bridge or smooth or dramatize them.

---

[5] "Theory in the study of religion in late antiquity" also delimits the task as mainly engaging North American scholarship since "late antiquity" tends to represent a largely North American reorientation away from "patristics" – one tied closely to a particular set of methodologies, as Anthony Kaldellis notes. Kaldellis, "Late antiquity dissolves," *Marginalia Review of Books*, September 18, 2015.

[6] These strands – gender/representation, Foucault/defamiliarization, postcolonialism/the global – are artificially separated to highlight the different dilemmas and conundrums undergirding them. Readers will no doubt notice this artificiality as they read and find returns, overlaps, and continuities across sections. These are mostly by design.

In Clark's work (beginning in the late 1970s), we see her wrestling with a knot of questions about gender, language/representation, and what we might call "thereness." How to "read" bodies in literature, how to situate their signs and meanings in their historical settings, and even to what extent those bodies are said to *be there*: these knots remain at the heart of so much scholarship. Likewise, Clark's own early hopes and struggles with feminist historiography bear out across decades and under differently pressured circumstances. One question I ask: can feminist historiography withstand the weight of these cumulative changes in time and circumstance?

His work kicking off about two decades before Clark's, Peter Brown was motivated by the question of accounting for cultural difference, which his encounters with Michel Foucault's work informed. So Section 2 of this present Element wanders around in Foucault's long and prolific reception in the field: he is a figure of both inspiration and discontent. He is often the unnamed, taken-for-granted center of new epistemological considerations, and just as often a name that carries its own varied meanings apart from the specificity of his work. Additionally, considering Brown's rapturous storytelling skills as essential to his work, I discuss his style itself as part of a long, somewhat hushed lineage in the field, a lineage of lyrical historiography that has its own integrity and ethos.

The earliest of the figures discussed here, Marrou, began his work in the 1930s. Like the Augustine he was writing about, Marrou was trying to make sense of two worlds at odds with one another. A citizen of France, he felt acutely the crisis of France's war on colonized Algeria as he struggled to explain Augustine. We see Marrou's impulses live on in later desires to write a late antiquity more account-able to the global relations of empire, and this accountability has come mainly in the form of engagements with postcolonial theory. Yet many of the direct implications of these engagements remain tentative, and so in Section 3, I try to draw out and escalate the more distinct political and ethical possibilities of this work for living in and with (neo)colonialism now, including the ways it affects the very shape of the study of religion in late antiquity.

1 Gender, Difference, Thereness, and Representation

"Soon, my interest turned to women in early Christianity: but where to find them?" In a retrospective biographical essay written in 2015 (after her retire-ment), Elizabeth Clark describes her scholarship through the many unexpected turns of a woman scholar encountering the openings and foreclosures of academic life specific to the mid-twentieth century.[7] As an exceptional figure privy to certain positions so often prohibited to women, she was of course

---

[7] Elizabeth A. Clark, "The retrospective self," *Catholic Historical Review*, 101 (2015), 1–27, at 8.

surrounded by men, a circumstance that one could imagine carried some loneliness and haunting precarity. It was in this long moment, and associatively linked to her own women's rights activism, that she began the work that became *Jerome, Chrysostom, and Friends*.[8] In that book, Clark describes how certain women's education and wealth mitigated their low status as women and allowed them to be seen by elite men (at least occasionally) as worthy conversation partners – echoing Clark's own uncertain inclusion in the world of idea-making men.

Twenty years after *Jerome, Chrysostom, and Friends*, the question of "Where to find them?" became vexed. In "The Lady Vanishes" (1998), Clark charts how poststructuralist theories had unsettled what had become fundamentals of feminist historiography, primarily the notions of women's experience and finding women as actors in history. The phrase "real women" now appears in scare quotes and the singular issue that plagued, or at least problematized, historical work was that texts inevitably constructed and narrativized at least as much as they revealed. Moreover, there was no sure way to tell which was which: "[W]e deal, always, with representation."[9]

In "The Lady Vanishes," Clark is drawing largely on Roland Barthes, Jacques Derrida, and Joan Wallach Scott, all of whom work under the umbrella of ideas, thinkers, and texts we describe as "poststructuralism." Poststructuralism is most often what is implied, by shorthand, in evoking "theory." As the word suggests, poststructuralism is the name given to a series of efforts to destabilize the very dichotomized oppositions seen (in structuralist paradigms) as basic to human understanding.[10] These were also efforts to undermine naturalized foundational and authoritative claims in the name of what anxieties haunt them and what excesses or failures those claims create.

Also called the "linguistic turn" for its emphasis on the power of language to produce realities (rather than simply referring to them), poststructuralism is associated with killing off two darlings of modernism: the author and the subject.[11] The death of the subject, Clark notes, was a loss some feminist historians were unwilling to accept. Agency and self-determination, which defined the

---

[8] Elizabeth A. Clark, *Jerome, Chrysostom, and Friends: Essays and Translations*. 2nd ed. (Edwin Mellen Press, 1982).

[9] Elizabeth A. Clark, "The lady vanishes: Dilemmas of a feminist historian after the 'linguistic turn,'" *Church History*, 67 (1998), 1–31, at 30.

[10] While poststructuralism is often thought of as a "school" with clear adherents, that oversimplifies the work and trajectories of the writers involved since many of the associated writers – Julia Kristeva, Jacques Lacan, Roland Barthes – were, at different times and to different extents, invested in and building on structuralist paradigms. Of course, these brief summaries I am offering are also reductions of a complex network of thinkers and ideas.

[11] On the death of the subject, see Jacques Derrida, *Of Grammatology* (Johns Hopkins University Press, 1998). More on the death of the author in Section 2.

subject in the modern sense, were cardinal (white, bourgeois) feminist values.[12] Why take away what women had only just begun to claim for themselves?[13]

Clark was not the first scholar in the field with feminist commitments to find herself at odds with these pillar values of feminist historiography.[14] In Virginia Burrus's "The Heretical Woman As Symbol" (1991), Burrus expressly describes herself as cautioning other feminist historians against romanticizing the associations between heresy and women in heresiological literature, as if such descriptions of women might offer a history of women pushing back against patriarchy and orthodoxy.[15] As an alternative, she takes Alain Le Boulluec's recognition that heresy and orthodoxy are not obvious categories, but rather mutually constituted constructions, to the figure of the heretical woman.[16] Burrus's article is a search for the "historical circumstances that gave rise to women's supposed proclivity to heresy" and to better understand how feminized figures were props in community debates and social conflicts.[17] This article appears only a few years after Burrus's first monograph, *Chastity As Autonomy* which, in addition to the signaling of "autonomy" in the title, implies a much more encouraging picture of the relationship between texts and the social lives of ancient women.[18]

In both Burrus and Clark, then, we witness pivots between what has been called second-wave and third-wave feminism, the latter of which is often defined primarily with respect to poststructuralism.[19] This changed orientation

---

[12] For critiques and recalibrations of agency and autonomy/self-determination, see Judith Butler, "Beside oneself: On the limits of sexual autonomy," in *Undoing Gender* (Routledge, 2004), 17–39; Saba Mahmood, *The Politics of Piety: The Islamic Revival and the Feminist Subject* (Princeton University Press, 2005); Cressida J. Heyes, *The Anaesthetics of Existence: Experience at the Edge* (Duke University Press, 2020).

[13] Clark, "The lady vanishes," 3.

[14] Clark was breaking with the feminist social history that was thriving in the 1990s, as seen in the work of Elisabeth Schüssler Fiorenza, Antoinette Clark Wire, and Bernadette Brooten, for example, all of whom were making careers on feminist historical reconstruction of women's activity, agency, and experience in antiquity.

[15] Virginia Burrus, "The heretical woman as symbol in Alexander, Athanasius, Epiphanius, and Jerome," *Harvard Theological Review*, 84 (1991), 229–248.

[16] See Alain Le Boulluec, *La notion d'hérésie dans la littérature grecque, IIe–IIIe siècles* (Études Augustiniennes, 1985). Le Boulluec, as Burrus points out, is approaching the construction of orthodoxy and heresy as Michel Foucault approaches the genealogy of madness and reason as mutually constituting. Michel Foucault, *Madness and Reason: A History of Insanity in the Age of Reason* (Vintage, 1988).

[17] Burrus, "The heretical woman," 231.

[18] Virginia Burrus, *Chastity As Autonomy: Women in the Stories of the Apocryphal Acts* (Edwin Mellen Press, 1987).

[19] Feminism as a history of waves is a popular narrative, but not an unproblematic one. For one, as Clare Hemmings argues, the story of the waves presumes Black feminism and poststructuralism (for instance) as "outside" of feminism proper, only interjecting to offer complications to a more "original" feminism. Hemmings, *Why Stories Matter: The Political Grammar of Feminist Theory* (Duke University Press, 2011).

has, over time, filtered through the field generally (if unevenly), as a not-insignificant portion of the field now tends to train its collective gaze more on *gender* than *women*, on discourse and on cultural constructions of phenomena rather than their referential ground.[20]

While critiques of the category of "woman" did not originate with poststructuralism, academic queer theory (heavily indebted to poststructuralism) popularized this critique. Judith Butler's work, specifically *Gender Trouble: Feminism and the Subversion of Identity* and *Bodies That Matter: On the Discursive Limits of Sex*, is iconic for its theorizing of the performativity of gender and its deconstruction of the sex/gender distinction.[21] Butler's rethinking of gender as always a copy without an original, as a citation of a norm that makes possible the undermining of the norm, became both the subtext and instrument of much critical historical work.[22] Eve Kosofsky Sedgwick's *Epistemology of the Closet* is much less often cited in the field, perhaps because it is not offering an extractable concept like Butler's performative citations.[23] But it is no less important, no less compelling, especially for its disjoining of the normative alignments sex-gender-sexuality.[24]

The turn to discursive constructions of gender was about many things. Across academic fields, it signaled not only an indebtedness to queer theory but also a hope to move beyond the limitations and problems of "woman" – an essentializing and universalizing category.[25] In the study of religion in late antiquity, however, the turn to discursive constructions of gender paralleled other

---

[20] An interest in the social histories of women, as I will suggest in what follows, has certainly not evaporated by any means. Likewise, there have been integrations of the interests in feminist social reconstructions and queer theory in New Testament scholarship – for instance, in the work on Paul's letters by Joseph Marchal. See Marchal, *Appalling Bodies: Queer Figures before and after Paul's Letters* (Oxford University Press, 2019).

[21] Judith Butler, *Gender Trouble: Feminism and the Subversion of Identity* (Routledge, 1990) and *Bodies That Matter: On the Discursive Limits of Sex* (Routledge, 1996).

[22] For a sampling of work indebted to Butler on gender and sexual difference, see Daniel Boyarin, *A Radical Jew: Paul and the Politics of Identity* (University of California Press, 1997); Virginia Burrus, *Begotten Not Made: Conceiving Manhood in Late Antiquity* (Stanford University Press, 2000); Stephanie Cobb, *Dying to Be Men: Gender and Language in Early Christian Martyr Texts* (Columbia University Press, 2008); Carly Daniel-Hughes, *The Salvation of the Flesh in Tertullian of Carthage: Dressing for Resurrection* (Palgrave, 2011); Kristi Upson-Saia, *Early Christian Dress: Gender, Virtue and Authority* (Routledge, 2011); Taylor Petrey, *Resurrecting Parts: Early Christians on Desire, Reproduction, and Sexual Difference* (Routledge, 2016). For essays on Butler's work on gender, performativity, and citationality relative to the field of religion at large, see Ellen T. Armour and Susan M. St. Ville (eds.), *Bodily Citations: Religion and Judith Butler* (Columbia University Press, 2006).

[23] It does appear, for instance, in Benjamin Dunning, *Specters of Paul: Sexual Difference in Early Christian Thought* (University of Pennsylvania Press, 2011).

[24] Eve Kosofsky Sedgwick, *Epistemology of the Closet* (University of California Press, 1990). See especially "Axiomatic," 1–65.

[25] For a sophisticated and fine-grained account of the relationship between feminism and queer theory as academic disciplines and the hopes of inclusivity attached to the movement from

deconstructive enterprises that sought to denaturalize the content of identities, revealing the norms and power relations organizing them. For instance, poststructuralism produced a profusion of scholarly literature on the "construction of Jewish and Christian identities" and an attention to the "production of difference" as a sociocultural process. One casualty of this approach was the notion of the "parting of the ways" between Judaism and Christianity, typically imagined as a distinct historical moment in which two legibly separate religious entities emerged (even though there was no agreement on when this moment occurred).[26] Judaism and Christianity were alternatively being reenvisioned as ongoing, unfinished projects, always articulating themselves in relationship to one another, ultimately sharing rhetorical and social processes, and drawing from similar (if not identical) traditions in the process.

Gender itself was crucial to instantiations of social and cultural difference: Cynthia Baker's *Rebuilding the House of Israel*, for instance, contends that rabbinic texts circumscribed women's bodies and sexuality, especially as women moved in various spaces: it is not that Jewish women were relegated to only domestic, private spheres; it is rather that women were embodiments of the house.[27] But, for Baker, these texts reflect social and economic anxieties, including around Roman imperialism and the threat "foreignness" presented for Jewish cultural identity.[28] Gender and ethnicity worked in tandem.

Thus these forms of social difference were understood both to rely on gender and to operate analogically to it. "Difference" with respect to Judaism and Christianity paralleled the notion of "sexual difference," a term issuing from psychoanalytically inflected feminist theory.[29] As it appeared in the work of philosopher Luce Irigaray and historian Joan Wallach Scott, "sexual difference" implies an irreducible psychic relationship of otherness, an unresolvable dilemma, in which gender is the "attribution of meaning to something that always eludes definition."[30] In Irigaray, it also implies biological/anatomical

---

"women" to "gender" as an analytic object, see Robyn Wiegman, *Object Lessons* (Duke University Press, 2012), 36–136.

[26] For example, Daniel Boyarin, *Border Lines: The Partition of Judeao-Christianity* (University of Pennsylvania Press, 2006); Adam Becker and Annette Yoshiko Reed (eds.), *The Ways That Never Parted: Jews and Christians in Late Antiquity and the Early Middle Ages* (Fortress Press, 2007); Eric Smith, *Jewish Glass and Christian Stone: A Materialist Mapping of the "Parting of the Ways"* (Routledge, 2017); Ra'anan Boustan and Joseph E. Sanzo, "Christian magicians, Jewish magical idioms, and the shared magical culture of late antiquity," *Harvard Theological Review*, 110 (2017), 217–240.

[27] Cynthia M. Baker, *Rebuilding the House of Israel: Architectures of Gender in Jewish Antiquity* (Stanford University Press, 2002).

[28] Baker, *Rebuilding the House of Israel*, 1–15.

[29] On the genealogy and problems of the term "sexual difference," see Dunning, *Specters of Paul*, 15–16.

[30] Joan Wallach Scott, *The Fantasy of Feminist History* (Duke University Press, 2011), 5–7.

referents.[31] Ben Dunning's *Specters of Paul*, for instance, takes up sexual difference to add nuance to the debates on Paul and gender, which have, in feminist scholarship, typically focused on the clear androcentrism and misogyny in the letters. Dunning, on the other hand, follows the unresolved and unresolvable conundrum of sexual difference through Paul and his readers.

The emphasis on "difference" in studies of cultural identity belies the fact that so much scholarship on constructions of Jewish and Christian identities was attempting to honor the blur and connectedness between Judaism and Christianity.[32] The question was not just how to honor the blur and connectedness, however, but how to do so while also accounting for the ways that claims to certain social identities can support or enact violence. Thus Christian representations of Jews, who were so often props for Christian self-definition, came under particular scrutiny. Susanna Drake's *Slandering the Jew*, for instance, follows the stereotype of the "carnal Jew" as it not only fortified Christian self-understanding but also shaped Christian engagement with scripture in late antiquity. For Drake, this sexualized invective also associatively linked Jewishness to heresy in order to delineate a proper Christianness, imagined as purged of any "outside" influences. What is "outside," however, is exactly what is in question. Drake, drawing from postcolonial theorists Homi Bhabha and Ann Laura Stoler, argues that such purity politics are best understood as muscular responses to a hybrid, colonial context.[33]

Drake's work demonstrates the heightened focus, arriving with poststructuralism, on the violence of normative reality construction. Her book, however, is also illustrative of the related conundrum of how to articulate precisely what the effects of violent texts or representations might be, how *material* those effects are.[34] Does violent language suggest social violence on the part of individuals speaking it? That question is too small, according to Drake: imperial legislation that variously propagated Jewish stereotypes and claimed protections for Jewish social spaces illustrates for Drake that discursive violence was not

---

[31] Luce Irigaray, *An Ethics of Sexual Difference*, Carolyn Burke and Gillian Gill, trans. (Cornell University Press, 1983); *Speculum of the Other Woman*, Gillian Gill, trans. (Cornell University Press, 1985). *Cultural* difference owed much of its epistemology to psychoanalytic theory too, especially because psychoanalytic theory had such a central place in the postcolonial and/or anticolonial work of Frantz Fanon, Homi Bhabha, and others. More on these figures in Section 3.

[32] "Difference" was additionally a keyword for making sense of Christian incoherence, for instance, and to try to neutralize the ideologically weighted social fractures implied by heresy/orthodoxy discourse. On the narrative management of intra-Christian difference, see Karen L. King, "Factions, diversity, multiplicity: Representing early Christian differences for the 21st century," *Method and Theory in the Study of Religion*, 23 (2011), 216–237.

[33] Susanna Drake, *Slandering the Jew: Sexuality and Difference in Early Christian Texts* (University of Pennsylvania, 2013), introduction.

[34] Additionally, see Ra'anan S. Boustan, Alex P. Jassen, and Calvin J. Roetzel (eds.), *Violence, Scripture, and Textual Practice in Early Judaism and Christianity* (Brill, 2010).

abstract.[35] What is more, discursive violence is not simply a matter of words versus deeds: "To comprehend the anti-Jewish violence of this era, we must first understand the 'representability' of Jewish life in early Christian discourses."[36] Anti-Jewish rhetoric facilitated an atmosphere of anti-Jewish violence.[37] "The discourses of stereotype, name-calling, and sexual slander examined here functioned not merely as linguistic devices of ancient invective but as performative acts that themselves produced reality for late ancient Jews and Christians."[38]

There is no question about the long arc of anti-Jewish and anti-Semitic violence that Christianity has rationalized from within itself. However, the heaviness of that history also can create a kind of epistemological overreach, a sense that anti-Judaism is the primary way in which all late ancient Christian engagements with Jewish traditions should be framed, as Jennifer Knust argues. Knust plays out the history and meanings of the veneration of the Maccabean martyrs by Christians in late antiquity, wondering if perhaps the scholarly tendency to read all instances of Christians taking up Jewish figures as appropriative means that we also miss instances in which they represented more shared and mutual relations.[39] Knust describes this tendency through queer theorist Eve Sedgwick's diagnosis of "paranoid readings," an affective (non-pathologizing) description of the overwhelming orientation of critique issuing from the "hermeneutics of suspicion."[40] "Paranoid Reading and Reparative Reading, or You're So Paranoid, You Probably Think This Essay Is about You," which appears in Sedgwick's book *Touching Feeling* (one of the books that kicked off "the affective turn"), questions the dominance of the "highly

---

[35] Drake, *Slandering the Jew*, 99–106.   [36] Drake, *Slandering the Jew*, 103.

[37] Likewise, on the relationship between rhetorical and real (historical) Jews/real Jewish-Christian relations, see Andrew Jacobs, *Remains of the Jew: The Holy Land and Christian Empire in Late Antiquity* (Stanford University Press, 2003), 207–208.

[38] However, Drake does not end with the ultimacy or totalizing effects of violence. She draws from Judith Butler's book *Excitable Speech: A Politics of the Performative* (Routledge, 1997) to offer the possibility that these kinds of interpellational injuries can also be "the site of subversion and resistance." Quoting Butler, these rhetorical forms of violence "can produce a scene of agency from ambivalence, a set of effects that exceed the animating intentions of the call." Drake, *Slandering the Jew*, 104.

[39] Jennifer Knust, "Jewish bones and Christian Bibles: The Maccabean martyrs in Christian late antiquity," presented at the Christianity Seminar of the Westar Institute, Santa Rosa, California, 2015. Compatibly, see Maia Kotrosits, *Rethinking Early Christian Identity* (Fortress Press, 2015) on how scholars' concerns about supersessionism, while obviously legitimate, can blot out possibilities for other readings of New Testament and related texts, including readings that demonstrate the fullness of these texts' investment in Israelite/Judean diasporic culture.

[40] Eve Kosofsky Sedgwick, *Touching Feeling: Affect, Pedagogy, Performativity* (Duke University Press, 2003). Sedgwick, in all of her work, built theoretical concepts from the idiosyncrasies of her experiences and relationships, as well as her sharp observations of the acute and diffuse forces of normative cultures.

compelling tracing-and-exposure project" with respect to systemic violence, not to deny that violence exists, but rather to ask, "What does knowledge *do*?"[41]

> [Paul] Ricoeur introduced the category of the hermeneutics of suspicion to describe the position of Marx, Nietzsche, Freud, and their intellectual offspring in a context that also included such alternative disciplinary hermeneutics as the philological and theological "hermeneutics of recovery of meaning." His intent in offering the former of these formulations was descriptive and taxonomic rather than imperative. In the context of recent U.S. critical theory, however, where Marx, Nietzsche, and Freud by themselves are taken as constituting a pretty sufficient genealogy for the mainstream of New Historicist, deconstructive, feminist, queer, and psychoanalytic criticism, to apply a hermeneutics of suspicion is, I believe, widely understood as a mandatory injunction rather than a possibility among other possibilities. (124–5)

Sedgwick notes the loss of other critical positions with the prestige of such critical paranoia, as well as the irony that few have ever interrogated it: "The imperative framing will do funny things to a hermeneutics of suspicion."[42]

The question of how "paranoid" our readings should be, and whether our attunement to violence is also a crowding out of other forms of knowing, or other historical possibilities, is an important one that ultimately frames a lot of the field. Clark's and Burrus's apparent pessimism certainly has not disappeared social histories of women – or children, whose representation in ancient literature is just as fraught.[43] In some cases, the task became to understand the gaps

---

[41] See later in Section 1 for more on theories of affect.

[42] Sedgwick, *Touching Feeling*, 125. Sedgwick's book, and her emphasis on reparative practices/ positionings as counterpoint to paranoid ones, has been extremely popular across fields. Reparative readings and practices have held so much sway that they have received their own critiques, including Patricia Stuelke's *The Ruse of Repair: U.S. Neoliberal Empire and the Turn from Critique* (Duke University Press, 2021). Importantly, *Touching Feeling* was questioning disciplinary consensus-formation and the truth value taken on by certain epistemological modes above others:

> I suppose this ought to seem quite an unremarkable epiphany: that knowledge does rather than simply is it is by now very routine to discover. Yet it seems that a lot of the real force of such discoveries has been blunted through the habitual practices of the same forms of critical theory that have given such broad currency to the formulae themselves. In particular, it is possible that the very productive critical habits embodied in what Paul Ricoeur memorably called the "hermeneutics of suspicion" – widespread critical habits indeed, perhaps by now nearly synonymous with criticism itself – may have had an unintentionally stultifying side effect: they may have made it less rather than more possible to unpack the local, contingent relations between any given piece of knowledge and its narrative/ epistemological entailments for the seeker, knower, or teller. (124)

This context for Sedgwick's essay is key, and her worries about the propagation and reproduction of critical habits without consideration of the force of their effects (including dispositional ones) have been influential for me, and, perhaps obviously, lives on in this present Element, among other places.

[43] See, for instance, Ross Shepard Kraemer's very pointed critique of Clark in *Unreliable Witnesses: Religion, Gender, and Religion in the Greco-Roman Mediterranean* (Oxford University Press, 2012).

and paradoxes in textual representations alongside other kinds of evidence to reconstruct more complicated (though not happy) pictures of social life.[44] Caroline Schroeder's *Children and Family in Late Antique Egyptian Monasticism* shows how children were present in various ways in monastic communities, but their presence was vexed and heavy as they disrupted so many monastic aspirations and self-understandings.[45] Sarit Kattan Gribetz sidesteps the long-running conundrum of whether women could be said to be authors and producers of texts. She does so by drawing from the evidence for women in monastic communities to speculate on the more secure possibility of women *readers*, specifically for the Nag Hammadi codices.[46]

Another, related question haunted by the hermeneutics of suspicion is whether to read instances in which gender is a source of play or ambiguity in late ancient literature as playful subversion or a reinscription of norms. While scholars such as Burrus and Peter Mena have read gender mutability in hagiographical texts as transgressive or full of possibility,[47] other scholars offer less hopeful assessments. Stephanie Cobb's *Dying to Be Men*, to give one example, argues via martyrological literature that Christian identity relied heavily on the culturally mainstream expectations of masculinity and virility in order to pronounce itself.[48] In this book, Cobb, like others, reads martyrdom literature for "narrative effects" rather than for historical phenomena. She also questions scholarship that associates mixed-gender presentation of some martyrs, such as the masculinized

---

[44] In addition to Kraemer's *Unreliable Witnesses*, examples of scholars navigating the challenges of representation and the desire for women's social history include Caroline T. Schroeder, "Women in anchoritic and semi-anchoritic monasticism in Egypt: Rethinking the landscape," *Church History*, 83 (2014), 1–17, which tries to reconcile the literary presence with the documentary absence of women in monasticism. See also Susan Hylen's *A Modest Apostle: Thecla and the History of Women in the Early Church* (Oxford University Press, 2015). Hylen reads the Acts of Paul and Thecla alongside 1 Timothy, and then literary representations of Thecla across late antiquity, to reconstruct the paradoxical social roles and expectations of women in Christian communities. See also Kim Haines-Eitzen, *The Gendered Palimpsest: Women, Writing, and Representation in Early Christianity* (Oxford University Press, 2011). Haines-Eitzen paints a social history of women in textual production. In some ways, Haines-Eitzen reiterates the poststructuralist textualization of bodies in a materialist vein, demonstrating how the representation of women was bound up in scribal practices. For a fusion of feminist questions and new philological questions of textual production, see Jennifer Knust and Tommy Wasserman, *To Cast the First Stone: The Transmission of a Gospel Story* (Princeton University Press, 2020), who write on the history of the pericope of the adulterous woman from the Gospel of John.

[45] Caroline Schroeder, *Children and Family in Late Antique Egyptian Monasticism* (Cambridge University Press, 2020). See also Maria Doerfler, *Jephthah's Daughter, Sarah's Son: The Death of Children in Late Antiquity* (University of California Press, 2020).

[46] Sarit Kattan Gribetz, "Women as readers of the Nag Hammadi codices," *Journal of Early Christian Studies*, 26 (2018), 463–494.

[47] Virginia Burrus, *The Sex Lives of Saints: An Erotics of Ancient Hagiography* (University of Pennsylvania Press, 2007). Peter Anthony Mena, *Place and Identity in the Lives of Antony, Paul, and Mary of Egypt: Desert As Borderland* (Palgrave Macmillan, 2019).

[48] Cobb, *Dying to Be Men*.

Perpetua, with a subversion of dominant notions of gender, since the operative logic is still a valorization of dominant forms of masculinity.[49]

Similarly, David Brakke's "The Lady Appears" addresses monastic sayings and stories about monks who are presumably men but are revealed in the end to "actually" be women. Brakke is not interested in the "positivist task for the actual motivations of real cross-dressing monks"; he is rather hoping to take Clark's cue and "explore the relationship between the literary and the social, the rhetorical and the real."[50] Like Cobb, Brakke ultimately finds these sayings and stories to reveal a valorization of masculinity as spiritual achievement, and women's spiritual achievement a tactic for shaming men. But compatible with Drake's description of discursive violence, Brakke also finds that such representations were tied to, if not responsible for, the material conditions of abandonment and legislation by men.

Brakke's piece in particular reminds us that, since the linguistic turn, while language could not be trusted to describe historical phenomenon in any self-evident fashion, language was still a trusted route – *the* trusted route – for revealing the metarealities of social and ideological forces. But analyses of metarealities will always bring with them material referents.[51] The "real" is never far behind. So the more interesting question may be what poststructuralist-informed accounts endowed with realness, or where the "real" stubbornly remained.

For example, if understandings of bodily life were recalibrated to reveal bodies as textualized products of their historical and cultural ecologies, bodily *experiences* such as desire or shame were nonetheless vividly present and immanently describable. In her 1993 article, "The Blazing Body," Patricia Cox Miller reads Jerome's letter to Eustochium as constructing an "erotics of asceticism" through a textualization of "the female body" as "burning with the signifiers of desire."[52] The desire, of course, is principally Jerome's. But in this article we also see that not everything is susceptible to textualization: while the lady vanishes, *someone* is still present, and even accessible, in and through the text. And that is Jerome himself: "However, Jerome's physical presence in

---

[49] Cobb specifically argues against Daniel Boyarin's book *Dying for God: Martyrdom and the Making of Christianity and Judaism* (Stanford University Press, 1999). Cobb, *Dying to Be Men*, 12.

[50] David Brakke, "The lady appears: Materializations of 'woman' in early monastic literature," in Dale B. Martin and Patricia Cox Miller (eds.), *The Cultural Turn in Late Ancient Studies: Gender, Asceticism, and Historiography* (Duke University Press, 2005), 25–39, at 26. See the Introduction for another account of cultural studies and theory in the field, one with overlaps and differences from the one I offer here.

[51] See Rey Chow, "The interruption of referentiality; or, Poststructuralism's outside," in *The Age of the World Target: Self-Referentiality in War, Theory, and Comparative Work* (Duke University Press, 2006), 45–70.

[52] Patricia Cox Miller, "The blazing body: Ascetic desire in Jerome's Letter to Eustochium," *Journal of Early Christian Studies*, 1(1993), 21–45, at 24.

the letter is very strong – much stronger, in fact, than Eustochium's – and, we shall see, he was not able to achieve the metaphorical closure for his body that he accomplished for Eustochium's."[53] Miller argues that Jerome's *body*, not just his "libido," remains recalcitrantly present in and despite the medium of the letter. His body cannot be textualized, hard as he might try.

In many cases, we might even say that in the wake of poststructurally informed readings of gender, while *women* vanished, leaving only traces, what appeared most concrete, in aggregate, was patriarchy, men's fantasies and desires, and even men "themselves." So much so that even textual instances of drag or gender queerness in ancient literature too become signs of patriarchy's ultimate triumph and the machinations of men. The problem is not the critical unveiling of patriarchy itself, but what – to follow Sedgwick's critique of "paranoid readings" – takes on epistemological weight in this unveiling. While savvy readers scoured texts to find, or distance us from, "real women," or warn that the barest hint of hope in literary women was "really" the puppet-mastery or hot flashes of men, we might want to ask how such binary framings crowd out other possibilities for reading gender in late ancient history. This is what Melissa Harl Sellew grapples with in her trans*-centered reading of the Gospel of Thomas, as she holds the masculinist priorities of the saying in Gospel of Thomas 114, in which Jesus promises to "make Mary male" so that she may enter the kingdom of God, in tension with other themes across the text that resonate more hopefully with trans* experience.[54] "I see an opening to a more constructive, trans-centred reading of the passage when we note that Jesus draws a small but clear pronominal distinction between himself and his *male* disciples: Mary will become a Living Spirit, resembling '*you males*,'" she writes.[55] Sellew finds that the Gospel of Thomas is actually quite coy about Jesus' gender and bodily presentation, leaving space for a self-understanding not quite so doggedly overwritten by them: "A reading that employs an explicitly trans-centred hermeneutic might allow us to see the gender of Jesus and of other Living Spirits as queered away from vectors of bodily difference."[56]

We have yet to see in a full way how the political exigencies, richness, and complexity of trans* experiences will affect the field's long-running explorations of gender in late antiquity.[57] We can already begin to see the way transness might recalibrate the terms of the explorations themselves: note how

---

[53] Miller, "The blazing body," 31.

[54] Melissa Harl Sellew, "Reading the Gospel of Thomas from here: A trans-centred hermeneutic," *Journal of Interdisciplinary Biblical Studies*, 1 (2020), 61–96.

[55] Sellew, "Reading the Gospel of Thomas," 86.

[56] Sellew, "Reading the Gospel of Thomas," 89.

[57] See the issue Trans*histories of *Transgender Studies Quarterly*, 5(2018), for some ways to think about the historicization of trans* identities in premodern periods.

the constant invoking of "real women" across scholarship (whether presumed historically present or absent) easily takes on transphobic resonances that haunt that task or at the very least unsettle it. Similarly unsettled is the strong analytical investment in gender presentation in critical scholarship and the concomitant identification of bodily presentation with gender identity. To start, we will need to read against textual ideology of the revelation of realness – including, importantly, resisting the lures of the dramatized unveiling of the "true" gender of historical subjects. It is perhaps the case then that trans* studies and trans* experiences will change the stakes of the real, the present, the material that have accompanied the questions around women and gender in history for decades.[58] "Representation" itself looks different through the lens of the paradoxes of trans* visibility, in which increased "positive" representation coincides with increased susceptibility to material violence.[59]

To return, however, to the centrality of patriarchy (as we often do): patriarchy as *the* organizing hierarchy for social relations and the telos of gendered enactments has other complications. For one it can hide or at least downplay the ways gender functions within colonial and racializing schemas, as I will discuss further on. Another complication attending the inevitability of patriarchy is that it contains within it some of the unresolved attachments and hopes of second-wave feminism: it seems to register the impossibility of liberatory readings, readings that are perhaps, at heart, still appealing or desired. Even more, it signals the replacement of ancient historical women's agency with a certain aggrandized *contemporary critical agency*. Feminist historians, in contrast to their historical subjects, ostensibly have the power of representation in their own hands: the power to correct, or at least rewrite, the record.

This felt power of critical agency often emanated, aura-like, from the feminist historian of late antiquity herself. This is especially true of the ones who had managed, like Clark, to climb their way to the upper echelons of the academy (and with the bruises to show for it). Carly Daniel-Hughes suggests just that in

---

[58] See, for instance, the work of Gayle Salamon, especially *Assuming a Body: Transgender and the Rhetorics of Materiality* (Columbia University Press, 2010).

[59] Reina Gossett, Eric A. Stanley, and Johanna Burton, eds., *Trap Door: Trans Cultural Production and the Politics of Visibility* (MIT Press, 2017). This book deals exactly with this contradiction through trans art, visual cultures, and visual grammars.

> In today's complex cultural landscape, trans people are offered many "doors" – entrances to visibility, to resources, to recognition, and to understanding. Yet, as so many of the essays collected here attest, these doors are almost always also "traps" – accommodating trans bodies, histories, and culture only insofar as they can be forced to new hegemonic modalities … Yet in addition to *doors* that are also always *traps,* there are trapdoors, those clever contraptions that are not entrances or exits but secret passageways that take you someplace else, often someplace yet unknown. (xxiii)

"Mary Magdalene in the Fantasy Echo."[60] Drawing from Joan Wallach Scott's *Fantasy of Feminist History*, Daniel-Hughes reflects on the psychosocial dynamics of feminist historiography on Judaism and Christianity that took place during the late 1990s, when she started graduate school. She recounts the felt efficacy of feminist historiography: its urgent necessity and identifications produced a sense of solidarity, an imagined collective of mutual interest, even across time. The women of history and the women who studied history often fused, and social affections and attachments – as well as historical reconstructions – were born in the process. But this fantasy of solidarity faltered as feminism could not forestall the regular hierarchies and destructive interpersonal dynamics of academic life, even (sometimes especially) between feminist academics. Daniel-Hughes quotes Sara Ahmed: "There is no guarantee that in struggling for justice we ourselves will be just."[61] Neither could the fantasy of almost limitless agency that accompanied feminist historiographical and critical practices hold, not forever. Daniel-Hughes recounts how her admired advisor, Karen King, a scholar known for her historical restraint and who occupied the oldest chair at the world's richest and most famous university, was not protected from snickering accusations of "bad history" tied to her feminist commitments.

Feminist historiography is no less socially and affectively powerful four decades after it gained real power in the field. Blossom Stefaniw's recent article, "Feminist Historiography and Uses of the Past," written with the compelling urgency of a manifesto, circulated with fervor across social media platforms and reupped the felt sense of solidarity and yearning that Daniel-Hughes so delicately recounts.[62] Stefaniw's article both raises the existential disciplinary stakes and updates the possibilities of feminist historiography through recourse to critical race theory. In the process, she suggests how feminist historiography should be a diligent correction of embarrassing falsehoods, as well as a practice of counternarrative:

> The act of telling, archiving, collecting, and persistently repeating counter-stories must be the central act of feminist historiography. If the received [patriarchal] story is manifestly false, then it is impossible to see what academic merit or intellectual value there could possibly be in continuing to repeat that story. In other words, all historiography must be feminist and anti-racist historiography to have a hope in hell of being accurately human historiography. (282)

---

[60] Carly Daniel-Hughes, "Mary Magdalene in the fantasy echo: Reflections on the feminist historiography of early Christianity," in Taylor Petrey, Carly Daniel-Hughes, Benjamin Dunning et al. (eds.), *Re-making the World: Christianity and Categories, Essays in Honor of Karen L. King* (Mohr Siebeck, 2019), 135–159.

[61] Daniel-Hughes, "Mary Magdalene in the fantasy echo," 151. Sara Ahmed, *Living a Feminist Life* (Duke University Press, 2017), 6.

[62] Blossom Stefaniw, "Feminist historiography and uses of the past," *Studies in Late Antiquity*, 4 (2020), 260–283.

Feminist historiography then, for Stefaniw, is about representation as comprehensive historical renarration rather than an address to the more constricted themes of sexuality or the construction of gender.

In this piece, Stefaniw is frank about the disillusionment with which she is struggling: the depressing failure of real progress for women in the academy, the ongoing conservatism of the field, and the realities of harassment and discrimination. "It is not the case that we are on a steady course of progress towards justice and righteousness."[63] Her disillusionment resolves itself in the methodological orientation laid out in the piece: "We do feminist historiography in the face of persistent institutionalized misogyny in the very academy which is supposed to be our intellectual home, where academic patriarchy is domestic violence. How do we live and think around, through, and beyond such intimate wickedness?"

Stefaniw's rhetorical turns are equal parts poetic and provocative. For her, "patriarchy is permanent ... It is the fundamental structure of thought and action, farther down and farther back even than racism or violence or contempt for the poor."[64] To make this statement, she quotes evolutionary theory. I am less interested at the moment in assessing the truth value of this statement (or the recourse to evolutionary theory) than I am in the way Stefaniw toggles between underlining the social and biological vastness of patriarchy – its utter intractability – and calling her readers to action via (expanded) feminist historiographical practices. Patriarchy is the original human condition, but men and women engaged in the practice of writing history differently can overcome it.[65]

Part of the visceral power of Stefaniw's piece is the sheer intensity of its metaphors (the academy is both "home" and a scene of "domestic violence"). We can, though, imagine her essay as having a relationship to the paradoxes of belonging, the contradictions of clear privilege and limited agency, that Clark was working out with some careful understatement decades before. Despite Stefaniw's frustration with certain kinds of "feminist critical theory," by which she seems to mean theories of social construction, there is still hope for her, even potentially *progress*, in and through *certain kinds* of critical work, to resolve misogyny and conservatism in the academy and beyond.

For Stefaniw it would seem the failure of feminist historiography of the past to accomplish real change, despite its institutionalization, was because it was not comprehensive enough or not universally taken up. She offers "critical race theory" as a kind of additive solution to (white) feminist historiography's limits

---

[63] She adds, "Black intellectuals have known that for a long time" (263).

[64] Stefaniw, "Feminist historiography," 265.

[65] "Men and women" is Stefaniw's framing. She emphasizes this work must not only be done by women.

and a way of expanding its reach, echoing the way Black studies, Black feminist, womanist, and intersectional analyses often figure in white scholarship/fields – in part, to protect such fields/scholarship from critique.[66] We may want to entertain the possibility, with Daniel-Hughes, that the power and efficacy of academic feminist historiography (distinct, for right now, from feminism as such) was always, in part, expressive. That is, it was always a matter of navigating and surviving the conditions and paradoxes of academic women's lives. This does not undermine the value of feminist historiography (in which I am also invested), nor is it to suggest subjective or psychosocial reverberations of scholarship are specific to feminist historiography – clearly they are not.[67] It is, however, to observe a potentially detrimental equation between the expressive allure/cathartic effects of certain modes of feminist historiography and their political potency. It is detrimental in part because it allows its partakers to imagine and feel their own upward mobility and institutional security *as a form of justice*, thus prohibiting more comprehensive structural critiques and extending attachments to the very institutions doing harm.

I linger on Stefaniw's piece because it so fully illustrates a feminist histori-ography not just dealing with crises, but itself in crisis, and feeling the accruing burden of so many social and institutional forces and desires. I also linger there because of its expressive allure. It illustrates how feelings do their own import-ant social and political work.

This second point is the basic premise of affect theory, and it is (in part) another intellectual legacy of feminism in its affinities and entwinements with queer theory and philosophy. Sara Ahmed and Ann Cvetkovich, central thinkers in cultural studies, both explicitly link their interest in the social life of emotions and the politics of felt experience with feminist politics.[68] For studies in religion in

---

[66] More on this point in the Conclusion. Stefaniw's casting of racism as a "parallel" but secondary condition to patriarchy signals this and signals the piece as written for a white feminist audience. Some of the writers she names also do not fit under "critical race theory" per se – the work of Saidiya Hartman, for instance. On the logic of "curricular solutionism" that funds institutional interest in minoritized fields such as women's studies and ethnic studies, see Rey Chow, *A Face Drawn in Sand: Humanistic Inquiry and Foucault in the Present* (Columbia University Press, 2021), introduction. Chow writes that "these other forms of knowledge are in effect made to shoulder what might be called the white academy's burden (of filth and guilt). For precisely that reason, within the knowledge economy of the university they are often perceived as lacking the prestige and respectability of the classical disciplines. After all, they have been brought in as a kind of cleaning service" (20).

[67] Nearly all my work addresses the psychosocial and affective valences and subtexts of scholarship.

[68] As Ann Cvetkovich writes in *Depression: A Public Feeling* (Duke University Press, 2012), "The affective turn also doesn't seem particularly new to me because the Public Feelings project represents the outcome of many years of engagement with the shifting fortunes of the feminist mantra that 'the personal is political' as it has shaped theoretical and political practice and their relation to everyday life" (8). See also, for instance, Sara Ahmed's *Cultural Politics of Emotion*

late antiquity, however, uptakes of affect theories have generally leaned more toward a "new materialist" orientation, even when engaging, say, Sara Ahmed. It is worth asking how these engagements metabolize and perhaps redirect some of the long-held questions and conundrums issuing from feminist historiography.

Affect and new materialist theories arrived together on the scene in cultural studies and philosophy as a counterpoint and redress to the linguistic turn. Consequently they offered a bit of an exit strategy for, or at least a detour around, the ultimacy of language and impasses of representation.[69] Affect and new materialism, as what we might call theories of immanence, generally leaned into ontology and phenomenology. Whether conceptualized as emotion or as an impersonal force and felt intensity that named emotions only attempt (and fail) to capture, affect has become a way of talking about embodiment and social relationships in their immediacy.[70] New materialist theories, which loosened the subject/object distinction and distributed agency beyond the human will and into a world of human and nonhuman, organic and nonorganic actors, has all but dropped questions of linguistic mediation in favor of a richly described animated and dynamic ecology of relations.[71]

Affect and new materialism fit neatly within some of the long-held interests of scholars of religion in late antiquity, namely sense experience and material culture.[72] They also enabled different kinds of pictures of ancient life, mainly

---

(Routledge, 2004), which contains a chapter called "Feminist attachments," and her book *The Promise of Happiness* (Duke University Press, 2010), which contains a chapter called "Feminist killjoys."

[69] See Maia Kotrosits, *The Lives of Objects: Material Culture, Experience, and the Real in the History of Early Christianity* (University of Chicago Press, 2020), introduction.

[70] Characterizations of affect and its attendant theories abound. I have written my own version with respect to biblical studies in *How Things Feel: Affect Theory, Biblical Studies, and the (Im) Personal*. Research Perspectives in Biblical Interpretation (Brill, 2016). You can get a sense of the variety and incoherence of "affect theory," even in its earlier stages, through *The Affect Theory Reader*, Melissa Gregg and Gregory J. Seigworth, eds. (Duke University Press, 2010). By now the field of affect studies is more or less as wide and dispersed as affect itself. Probably the earliest entry of any "affect theory" into studies of religion in late antiquity was Virginia Burrus's *Saving Shame: Martyrs, Saints, and Other Abject Subjects* (University of Pennsylvania Press, 2013), which draws from Sedgwick's *Touching Feeling* and treats affect more as emotion.

[71] For instance (with an eye toward variety and influence): Jane Bennett's *Vibrant Matter: A Political Ecology of Things* (Duke University Press, 2010), Bruno Latour, *We Have Never Been Modern* (Harvard University Press, 1993), and Eduardo Kohn, *How Forests Think: Toward an Anthropology beyond the Human* (University of California Press, 2013). The overlapping motivations for new materialist theories include a sharpened ecological sensitivity (in part, related to ecological damage), desires to bridge the humanities with the "hard" sciences, worries about anthropocentrism, and a hope to reclaim wonder about the world.

[72] See, for instance, Jennifer Knust, "Miscellany manuscripts and the Christian canonical imaginary," in Claudia Moser and Jennifer Knust (eds.), *Ritual Matters: Material Remains and Ancient Religion* (University of Michigan Press, 2017). Knust takes up the object-oriented ontology of Bruno Latour. For a new materialist-ecological reading of late ancient Christian texts, see Virginia

because of their different assumptions about power, sociality, agency, and embodiment. While identity and its construction had been analytical focal points for decades in the field, theories of affect saw bodies and selves as forming felt affiliations or as parts of shifting assemblages.[73] In Gilles Deleuze and Félix Guattari, the social is assembled in and through flows, intensities in and across bodies, binding collectives in not always predictable patterns. Power is a given body's *capacity*.[74] This is a very different story about power than ideological models, which figure power as oppressive/repressive, and even slightly different from Foucauldian models, which figure power as constituting worlds at an epistemological level to the degree that resistance, too, is always relationally bound to power.[75] For Deleuze and Guattari, assemblages are driven not by power but by

---

Burrus, *Ancient Christian Ecopoetics: Cosmologies, Saints, Things* (University of Pennsylvania Press, 2018). Cavan Concannon and C. Mike Chin have made the most pronounced gestures in the direction of "new materialism." Cavan Concannon's *Assembling Early Christianity: Trade, Networks, and the Letters of Dionysios of Corinth* (Cambridge University Press, 2017) takes up Latour's actor-network theory, as well as the assemblage theory of Gilles Deleuze. Chin takes up new materialism less out of an interest in theories of objects and more out of an interest in the poetry and animacy of objects on their own terms, given his artist practices in object and puppet theatre. See "Cosmos," in Catherine Michael Chin and Moulie Vidas (eds.), *Late Ancient Knowing: Explorations in Intellectual History* (University of California Press, 2015), 99–116, and "Apostles and aristocrats," in Catherine Michael Chin and Caroline T. Schroeder (eds.), *Melania: Early Christianity through the Life of One Family* (University of California Press, 2017), 19–33, as well as his review of S. Rebecca Martin and Stephanie M. Langin-Hooper (eds.), *The Tiny and the Fragmented: Miniature, Broken, or Otherwise Incomplete Objects in the Ancient World* (Oxford University Press, 2018). *Bryn Mawr Classical Review,* December 2020.

[73] See my own shift along these lines in Kotrosits, *Rethinking Early Christian Identity: Affect, Violence, and Belonging* (Fortress Press, 2015). Brian Massumi first articulated a discontent with identity construction which imagined subject pinned to a solid, immobile grid. After years of talk in cultural studies about power as iterative, as (for instance) gendered selves built from ritualized repetitions, Massumi's work sought to theorize *movement*. Massumi, *Parables for the Virtual: Movement, Affect, Sensation* (Duke University Press, 2002). One can also see in this book, however, an engagement with the so-called hard sciences, in order to articulate the sciences more capaciously to include relation, and the reclaimed relationship to wonder that is so prevalent of cultural studies work in this arena.

[74] For a succinct description of Deleuze and Guattari's understanding of power and how it relates to Foucault's see *A Thousand Plateaus*, Brian Massumi (trans.) (Athlone Press, 2001), xvii. See also the conversation between Foucault and Deleuze, 'Intellectuals and power', in D. F. Bouchard (ed.), *Language, Counter-memory, and Practice: Selected Essays and Interviews* (Cornell University Press, 1997).

[75] See Michel Foucault, *The History of Sexuality Volume 1: An Introduction* (Vintage Press, 1990), 94–96, for a programmatic description of Foucault's concept of power. On resistance:

> Where there is power, there is resistance, and yet, or rather consequently, this resistance is never in a position of exteriority in relation to power. Should it be said that one is always "inside" power, there is no "escaping" it, there is no absolute outside where it is concerned because one is subject to the law in any case? Or that, history being the ruse of reason, power is the ruse of history, always emerging the winner? This would be to misunderstand the strictly relational character of power relationships. Their existence depends on a multiplicity of points of resistance: these play the role of adversary, target, support, or handle in power relations. (95)

desire, and so they are characterized by variability. That variability can be intensified ("deterritorialized") or it can be capped or managed ("reterritorialized") by the
usual instruments of power, but it cannot be eliminated.[76] As opposed to hard and
instantiated structures of power, the heart of social life in this case became uneasy
potential, movement, and change.

It is this understanding of bodies and power that Michael Muhammad Knight
leverages in his reconsideration of depictions of Muhammad in the literature of
early Islam.[77] Knight observes the way the body of Prophet Muhammad and its
traces – his heart, his fingernails, his sweat, his saliva – comprise an extended
and distributed corporeality through the radiant and propitious energy of *baraka*. For Knight, Muhammad's body, as assemblage, expands and contracts in
its links to other bodies, often through consumption (drinking blood or urine) or
contact, and enhances the capacities of the bodies he joins, through healing, for
instance. Knight principally shows how the energetic cogence of Muhammad's
body and its traces were managed via its gendered representation: its prophetic
capacities were a function of Muhammad's maleness.[78] This did not, though,
strictly limit the capacities and uptakes of Muhammad's radiant flow.[79]

Other scholars have read for the production, regulation, and management of
affect as a way of tying people together, sometimes in surprising ways or to
surprising ends. Abby Kulisz writes on Timothy I's Letter 59 (*Disputation with
the Caliph al-Mahdī*) within the cultural mix of Christians and Muslims in Baghdad
in the late eighth and early ninth centuries, demonstrating how Timothy's evocation
of the "book" (*ktābā*) shared by Christians and Muslims does affective work. Both
material and transcendent, and strategically vague in its referents of any particular
set of scriptures or practices, "book" in Timothy's letter works to bind Christian and
Muslims in affiliation while also separating them, through hostility, from Jews. This
is why, Kulisz argues, the *Disputation* should not be read through the lens of
"interfaith dialogue," which romanticizes the terms of affiliation between
Christians and Muslims in the letter.[80] Rather, Kulisz relies on Sara Ahmed's

---

[76] These concepts are discussed in Deleuze and Guattari, *A Thousand Plateaus*, and *Anti-Oedipus: Capitalism and Schizophrenia* (University of Minnesota Press, 1983). Michael Muhammad Knight provides clear descriptions of these concepts in the context of his work in *Muhammad's Body: Baraka Networks and the Prophetic Assemblage* (University of North Carolina Press, 2020), 9–15.

[77] Knight describes his genealogy as issuing from Muslim feminist scholarship (Julie Hammer, Aysha Hidayatullah) and studies of Muslim masculinities (Amanullah De Sondy, Zahra Ayubi). Knight explains that he was inspired to draw from Deleuze and Guattari by Alexander G. Weheliye's *Habeas Viscus: Racializing Assemblages, Biopolitcs, and Black Feminist Theories of the Human* (Duke University Press, 2014). See Knight, *Muhammad's Body*, 9.

[78] Knight, *Muhammad's Body*, 102–133.   [79] Knight, *Muhammad's Body*, 134–150.

[80] Abby Kulisz, "Sacred friendship, holy hatred: Christian-Muslim encounters in the book in the medieval Middle East." Doctoral dissertation. Indiana University. 2022, at 52–80.

understanding of affect's power as related to its "stickiness," its ability to form relationships, sometimes through "sticky objects," and through the erasure of the histories that produce felt experiences of people and objects.[81]

Also borrowing from Ahmed, Sarah Porter's analysis of the affective ecology of a cruciform church in fourth-century Antioch, a locale rife with theological disagreements, argues that the "reorientation [in Ahmed] to emotion as *practice* in addition to *feeling* means affect is accessible to historical inquiry and traceable through historical materials – or at least as accessible and traceable as other historical data."[82] She approaches the church through its sponsorship and construction by Meletios, an encomium for Meletios given by John Chrysostom in the church, and the mosaics that decorated it. In the process, she argues that the architecture "constructs a frightening 'outside,' and a secure 'inside,'" while Chrysostom's oration "elided histories of conflict by stoking love and unity in his listeners" and the mosaics "amplified pleasure and belonging." Porter writes, "Each event formed a node of pleasurable, powerful, affect that could consolidate the Meletian faction in Antioch."[83]

In these studies, the question of whether to name any individual act or representation as reiterative or subversive is almost beside the point, as is how any given individual identifies. What's more, theories of affect and new materialism sidestep both the valorization of agency and its problematization, since agency is more of a diffuse and distributed capacity with very uncertain effects in these theoretical frameworks. But affect and new materialist theories, as they appear in the field, triangulate another conundrum that has dogged so much scholarship of the past thirty years: the problem of textuality and the real. In each of these examples, texts are not treated as transparent sources of information, but they are treated as a given for the reconstruction of felt phenomenon, even as it is clear that texts' affective potency arrives through their representational work. As Cvetkovich describes her work in *An Archive of Feelings: Trauma, Sexuality, and Lesbian Public Cultures*, she organizes her book as "an exploration of cultural texts as repositories of feelings and emotions, which are encoded not only in the content of the texts themselves but in the practices that surround their production and reception."[84]

---

[81] Sara Ahmed, *The Cultural Politics of Emotion*. Ahmed produces a Marxist analysis of these sticky objects as fetish objects.

[82] Sarah Porter, "A church and its charms: Space, sffect, and affiliation in late fourth-century Antioch," *Studies in Late Antiquity*, 5(2021), 641–642.

[83] Porter, "A church and its charms," 642.

[84] Ann Cvetkovich, *An Archive of Feelings: Trauma, Sexuality, and Lesbian Public Cultures* (Duke University Press, 2007), 7.

The problem of the "real," however, perhaps arrives on another plane: is this description of felt experience *historical*? The fact that feeling is core to human experience and at the same time defies the laws of historical evidence means that chronicling affective forms and forces is both a necessary and an elusive historical project. In Cvetkovich's book, for instance, she embraces the ironies of writing about trauma. "Because trauma can be unspeakable and unrepresentable and because it is marked by forgetting and dissociation, it often seems to leave behind no records at all. Trauma puts pressure on conventional forms of documentation, representation, and commemoration."[85] So Porter's logic for what makes affect an historically viable object of analysis – that it is a practice and thus accessible through data – is of course salient. I wonder, however, if we lose more than we gain by pulling affect back from its importantly precarious place in relationship to what is properly considered the "historical."[86] Particularly because affect is, at least in the Deleuzian framework, impossible to capture, it is a fundamentally speculative enterprise to characterize its historical force. In any framework, felt experience challenges and upends our documentary and evidentiary historical habits. It reframes the long-standing tensions between the subjective and the historical and presses us, in its own way, to ask not only what we make of the body, of *bodies*, but how we come to know what and who is *there*.

2 Foucault and Defamiliarization, or "Keeping Late Antiquity Weird"

"I wish I had been one of the Seven Sleepers of Ephesus," Peter Brown writes with characteristic wistfulness.[87] This is how he begins *The Making of Late Antiquity* (1978), a book that tries to make sense of the watershed changes he and others saw in the third to fifth centuries. In the story of the Seven Sleepers, seven monks were spared persecution by hiding (and sleeping) in a cave, finally waking and startled to find a Christian empire two hundred years later. "This book is an attempt to enter into their surprise." Brown's renditions of the late Roman world have an uncanny feel, indebted (no doubt) to his lyricism and penchant for defamiliarizing locution. The uncanniness was distinctly part of his "method." "[W]hen I first began to think of the theme of body and society in Early Christianity, I did so because I was haunted by a sense of 'disturbing strange-ness,'" Brown writes, reflecting on the curiosities and experiences that generated

---

[85] Cvetkovich, *An Archive of Feelings*, 7.
[86] For my own leveraging of affect to ask what counts as real, as evidence, in historical work, see Kotrosits, *The Lives of Objects*.
[87] I am borrowing the phrase "Keeping Late Antiquity Weird" from Kristina Sessa. See her article by the same name from Studies in Late Antiquity, 6 (2022). See Peter Brown, *The Making of Late Antiquity* (Harvard University Press, 1978), 1.

his 1988 book *Body and Society*.[88] He recounts moving from Cairo to California, "equally exotic" locales for him, and experiencing the distinct dynamics of freedom and restriction at community swimming pools in each place. This visceral sense of strangeness that he felt while watching cultural others configure social and cosmic relationships through the activities and presentations of their bodies gave rise to the book. While heavily indebted to British anthropology (Mary Douglas, Edward Evans-Pritchard), which sought to discern cultural universes through their symbolic and social logics, Brown also found a catalyst for this project in Michel Foucault. Foucault's genealogical approach to history forcefully disrupted assimilations of the past to the present. "From then on, I could reach out and grasp a world restored, at last, to its full strangeness."[89]

Brown's indebtedness to Foucault is not very explicit, but it is legendary. Brown has recounted the minor exchanges and mutual interest between Foucault and himself, in what in the end feels a little like a story of missed connections.[90] Interestingly, what Brown gets from Foucault is not a set of propositions to be plugged into his reading of late ancient literature, but rather a *style of approach* that produces an uncanny wonder. One also cannot help but notice that Brown and Foucault are both exceptional storytellers who prize historical detail, but for whom historical precision is not the main point.

The life of Foucault in the field after Brown's work is extensive but sometimes hard to pin down. Foucault's influence across academic fields is massive, thoroughgoing, and unavoidable, but his relationship to the study of late antiquity has its own peculiarities since Foucault wrote specifically about late ancient figures and phenomena. While studies of religion in late antiquity saw similar post-Foucauldian epistemological shifts as in other fields – in the move to discursive analysis, in redescriptions of power as not only oppressive, but infusing society and forming subjects, for instance – the work engaging Foucault in this field has often met him more along historicist lines, evaluating to what extent Foucault's understandings of Augustine, Cassian, and so forth were accurate.[91]

Other work put his genealogical method into practice. Genealogy, for Foucault, was a historical approach that sought specifically to defamiliarize and denaturalize the present through tracking the conditional contingencies that make it possible,

---

[88] Peter Brown, *The Body and Society: Men, Women, and Sexual Renunciation in Early Christianity*. 20th anniversary ed. (Columbia University Press, 2008), xxii.

[89] Brown, *Body and Society*, xxxv–xxxvi.

[90] Peter Brown, Foucault's Confessions lecture series. May–June 2021. Rice University. May 6, 2021.

[91] In addition to those discussed further on, see Elizabeth Clark, "Foucault, the fathers, and sex," *Journal of the American Academy of Religion*, 56 (1988), 619–641. Virginia Burrus, *Begotten Not Made*. David Brakke, "Ethiopian demons: Male sexuality, the black-skinned other, and the monastic self," *Journal of the History of Sexuality*, 10 (2011), 501–535.

following disjoints and discontinuities over time, in contrast to a developmental approach or search for origins.[92] In one iteration, Karen King's *What Is Gnosticism?* traces the modern history of deployments of "Gnosticism" as a historical category, which, she observes, had the tacit goal of defining an idealized (normative) Christianity, even as the content of that Christianity changed.[93] King writes:

> By perceiving how thoroughly the study of Gnosticism is tied to defining normative Christianity, we have been able to analyze where and how the academic study of Gnosticism in the twentieth century reinscribes and reproduces the ancient discourse of orthodoxy and heresy. We can also see shifts in that discourse where modern discourses of historicism and colonialism have intersected it. Such shifts fit very comfortably into the pattern that Michel Foucault has led us to expect when examining the history of discourse. Rather than linear lines of causal continuity, we see substitutions, transformations, disjunctures, incompatibilities, and entanglements. Gnosticism was substituted for heresy as the object of the discourse. (218–19)

Even if genealogy is not widely "applied" in a strict sense, many stalwarts of the taxonomic impulse in the history of the study of late antiquity have come under scrutiny over the past few decades, informed by the broad Foucauldian wave of historicizing critique (e.g., "paganism," "magic," "religion"). Foucault's work also catalyzed a set of critical reorientations to authorship, a site of long-running interest and speculation in antiquity studies. His essay "What Is an Author?" argues that the name of the author is more than a proper name attached to a person: it has a taxonomic function with respect to texts, texts as "belonging to" X. At the same time, authors are produced by the very writing attributed to them, which creates a discourse that exceeds "their" texts. Further, the "author" actually belies the nature of writing, in which "the writing subject endlessly disappears."[94]

---

[92] Michel Foucault, "Nietzsche, genealogy, history," in *Language, Counter-memory, Practice*, 139–164.

[93] Karen L. King, *What Is Gnosticism?* (Belknap Press, 2005). Also working with Foucauldian genealogy is Judith Perkins's *The Suffering Self: Pain and Narrative Representation in the Early Christian Era* (Routledge, 1995), introduction. King also draws from French sociologist Pierre Bourdieu's very portable concept of habitus. See *The Logic of Practice* (Stanford University Press, 1980). Bourdieu has a life in late antiquity studies too that I will not address at length here, but see also Caroline T. Schroeder's *Monastic Bodies: Discipline and Salvation in Shenoute of Atripe* (University of Pennsylvania Press, 2007), Mike Chin's *Grammar and Christianity in the Late Roman World* (University of Pennsylvania Press, 2008), and Benjamin Dunning, *Aliens and Sojourners: Self As Other in Early Christianity* (University of Pennsylvania Press, 2009). Earlier than King's work on Foucault's author function is Andrew Jacobs, "'Solomon's salacious song': Foucault's author function and the early Christian interpretation of the Canticum Canticorum," *Medieval Encounters*, 4 (1998), 1–23. Jacobs suggests that the author function works to soften, constrain, or make more palatable especially edgy or problematic texts.

[94] Michel Foucault, "What is an author?" in *Language, Counter-memory, Practice*, 116.

Foucault suggests that modernity's interest in the author mimics a Christian exegetical interest in imposing unity on a lively and contradictory corpus.[95]

Scholars have routinely preoccupied themselves with sussing out, for instance, authentic letters from inauthentic letters, who "really" authored various texts, and why texts disparate in time and location and even content came to be connected by a name. The study of religion in late antiquity – Christianity in particular – has been especially overdetermined by the centrality of authors "themselves," as Ellen Muehlberger writes. She notes that the historical archive has been fundamentally shaped by this devotion to authors whose implicit authority carries over from the conceptualization of the field as "patristics."[96]

In many ways, authorship has been entangled in two other elements, authority and authenticity, as A. J. Berkovitz and Mark Letteney have observed.[97] Foucault provided ground for working out more candidly this long preoccupation in the field with authors, authenticity, and authority. Karen King, paralleling her genealogical approach to Gnosticism, suggests a close application of the principle of "author function" to ancient literature in order to better characterize the conditional nature, discursive peculiarities, and complex material circumstances of attribution in antiquity.[98] But for rabbinic texts, Martin Jaffee has shown, such an author function holds no sway as the compositional process and anthological style "points to a literary culture in which the minds and intentions of authors are displaced by the interpretive experiments that emerge among people engaged in mutual discourse over the shared texts."[99] This does not mean, Jaffee points out, that these texts are "authorless," but rather collectively authored. They are not completed in the writing but in their stretching out toward oral performance and recomposition.

Foucault is not alone in theorizing authorship. Jacques Derrida and Roland Barthes both figure in the "death of the author" as well, though their work on this is not as often discussed in the field.[100] Decades after the author's death, the

---

[95] Foucault, "What is an author?" 127–128.

[96] Ellen Muehlberger, "On authors, fathers, and holy men," *Marginalia Review of Books*, September 20, 2015.

[97] A. J. Berkovitz and Mark Letteney, eds., *Rethinking "Authority" in Late Antiquity: Authorship, Law, and Transmission in Jewish and Christian Tradition* (Routledge, 2018), introduction.

[98] Karen L. King, "'What is an author?' Ancient author function in the Apocryphon of John and the Apocalypse of John," in William Arnal et al. (eds.), *Scribal Practices and Social Structures among Jesus Adherents: Essays in Honour of John S. Kloppenborg* (Peeters, 2016), 15–42.

[99] Martin S. Jaffee, "Rabbinic authorship as a collective enterprise," in Charlotte Elisheva Fonrobert and Martin S. Jaffee (eds.), *The Cambridge Companion to the Talmud and Rabbinic Literature* (Cambridge University Press, 2007), 17–37, at 35.

[100] Though for an engagement with Roland Barthes on authorship and attribution, see Sacha Stern, "Attribution and authorship in the Babylonian Talmud," *Journal of Jewish Studies*, 45 (1994), 28–51. For summary of theoretical literature on authorship and its relationship to early Christian literature, see Greg Fewster, "Dying and rising with the author: Specters of Paul and the material text," in Clarissa Breu (ed.), *Biblical Exegesis without Authorial Intention? Interdisciplinary Approaches to Authorship and Meaning* (Brill, 2019), 149–183.

author has made a tentative and fragmented reappearance in the materiality and circulation of the text.[101] However, this post-deconstruction orientation has not quite found its way into late antiquity studies yet.

Foucault frames so much work in the field postulating the social and material vicissitudes of writing and books, though often only marginally so or between the lines. Blossom Stefaniw's *Christian Reading: Language, Ethics, and the Order of Things* does not engage Foucault specifically very often. It does, however, theorize grammar and reading as they produce subjects, it engages the analytics of episteme and genealogy, and it calls up Foucault's *The Order of Things: An Archaeology of the Human Sciences* in its title.[102] Matthew Larsen's *Gospels before the Book* proposes that modern assumptions about books and publication, as well as late ancient discourses about the authorship of the gospels, misapprehend the gospels (specifically, the Gospel of Mark) as finished and distinct works.[103] Here too, even as he takes Foucault's invitation to address writing in a historicized fashion with attention to historical disjuncture, and to detach authorship from the writing subject, Larsen cites Foucault explicitly at only two key moments, one in which he critiques Foucault's ostensible binary of authored and non-authored texts.[104] The other citation is of Foucault's description of the function of *hypomnemata*, unfinished "reminders" or notes, employed to describe the function of the Gospel of Mark.[105]

Foucault is regularly a site of dissatisfaction. Ellen Muehlberger argues with Foucault's incipient ideas about pastoral power.[106] Niki Kasumi Clements reads John Cassian not as the beginning of a new form of power, as Foucault reads him, but rather as a figure whose practices extend Foucault's work on ethical self-formation.[107] I have offered an alternative to the penetrative model of ancient sexuality prized by Foucault and David Halperin after him.[108] Likewise, an edited volume of collected essays, *Rethinking "Authority" in Late Antiquity*, expresses

[101] See, for instance, Jane Gallop, *The Deaths of the Author: Reading and Writing in Time* (Duke University Press, 2011) and my engagement with Gallop in *Rethinking Early Christian Identity*, chapter 7. See also Michal Beth Dinkler on "epistolary embodiment" in *Literary Theory and the New Testament*, 163–190, and Dinkler's elaboration of this concept in "Pauline epistles as affective technologies: Liberating literary form and the Letter to Philemon," *Biblical Interpretation*, 30 (2022), 556–577, which takes cues from affect theory and the Deleuzian "assemblage."

[102] Blossom Stefaniw, *Christian Reading: Language, Ethics, and the Order of Things* (University of California Press, 2019).

[103] Matthew D. C. Larsen, *Gospels before the Book* (Oxford University Press, 2018).

[104] Larsen, *Gospels before the Book*, 8.   [105] Larsen, *Gospels before the Book*, 144.

[106] Ellen Muehlberger, *Moment of Reckoning: Imagined Death and Its Consequences in Late Ancient Christianity* (Oxford University Press, 2019).

[107] Niki Kasumi Clements, *Sites of the Ascetic Self: John Cassian and Christian Ethical Formation* (University of Notre Dame Press, 2020).

[108] Kotrosits, "Penetration and its discontents: Greco-Roman sexuality, the Acts of Paul and Thecla, and theorizing eros without the wound," *Journal of the History of Sexuality*, 27 (2018), 343–366.

discontent that authority has been a primary way of understanding the function of attribution of authorship to ancient literature: it has been generally assumed that to append the name of a recognized authority figure to a text is to not only name a text in a tradition but also helps guarantee the text's survival. The thesis of this volume is that this understanding overshoots the evidence. The writers collectively suggest instead that authorship does not necessarily correlate to authority. The editors of the volume locate that correlation, the "reduction to authority," in the linguistic turn and Foucauldian assumptions about power. "We have become so aware of the tautology of 'power always wins out,' and the conviction that 'history is written by the winners' that alternative factors, those which do not fit neatly into a paradigm aimed at explicating systems of power, are marginalized, deemed irrelevant, or considered beneath the task of the historian."[109]

For Foucault, however, power is not localizable in something like "authority." It rather operates diffusely in and through practices, discourses, and institutions regardless of their social status. Likewise the tenet that history is produced by ruling classes or dominant entities is simply a basic supposition of social history. And importantly, the linguistic turn understood texts as fields of excess signification that always produced, in their excesses, their own subversions. My point is less to correct than to notice how "Foucault" and "Foucauldian" often operate (as Foucault himself obviously theorized) discursively in the field – in this case as ground for expressing discontent with totalizing paradigms of power. Foucault is a figure who exceeds his own corpus and who gets displaced by the interests with which he is metonymically associated. This is despite the fact (or maybe because) his work has enabled the field from its earliest glimmerings.

Late ancient Christian texts figure heavily in Foucault's intellectual life, especially in his later work, with respect to the history of sexuality, technologies of the self, and the arts of living.[110] Foucault concentrates his attention on late ancient Christianity most fully in what was published as his fourth volume of the *History of Sexuality*, which was met with interest, if also with controversy and disappointment.[111] For others, Foucault's later work in general, especially

---

[109] Berkovitz and Letteney, *Rethinking "Authority" in Late Antiquity*, 2.

[110] For a comprehensive mapping of Foucault's interests in Christianity, see Niki Kasumi Clements, "Foucault's Christianities," *Journal of the American Academy of Religion*, 89 (2021), 1–40.

[111] Michel Foucault, *The History of Sexuality Volume 4: Confessions of the Flesh*, ed. Frederic Gros, trans. Robert Hurley (Pantheon, 2021). Despite Foucault's hesitations about the work in this volume, it was finally edited and published posthumously in 2018 in French and in 2021 in English. See Daniel Boyarin and Elizabeth Castelli's introduction in "Foucault's 'The History of Sexuality'. The fourth volume, or, A field left fallow for others to till," *Journal of the History of Sexuality*, 10 (2001), 357–374, for a sense of some of the critiques, including that Foucault's genealogy does not include Jews or women.

its focus on ethics and the care of the self or transformation, seemed to veer away from the radicality of his early critique of institutions and governmentality (see *The Birth of the Prison, The Birth of the Clinic,* and *Madness and Civilization*) and even perhaps ended up resembling the values of neoliberalism he exposed in his work on biopower.[112]

Niki Kasumi Clements's extensive treatment of Foucault's work and its relationship to the history of Christianity has pushed back on these critiques. She recognizes some of the limits of Foucault's theories of self-government, given their reliance on the practices of elite, property-owning men of antiquity (as Foucault himself admits with disdain). She grants that Foucault's readings of ancient and late ancient writers sometimes rely on outdated and faulty assumptions about these texts. She nonetheless suggests a "charitable" engagement with the last decade of Foucault's work, one that recognizes its incompleteness as well as its potential relationship to Foucault's earlier work. She argues that this later work expands the "ethico-political range of possibilities for transformation of self and social norms in the history of Christianity."[113] In her book too, Clements argues vehemently against accusations that Foucault's later work is too friendly to neoliberal ideals.[114] Clements sees these gestures toward ethics and self-transformation as unambiguously positive, even liberatory. In the process, Clements finds, perhaps romantically, that both Cassian and Foucault offer an unfinished radicality that will bear out her own contemporary liberal/ progressive politics.[115]

Mira Balberg's *Purity, Body, and Self in Early Rabbinic Literature* has similarly drawn from Foucault's work on ethics and the self and done so from the perspective of rabbinic legal sources. "Rabbinic legislation, or *halakhah,*"

---

[112] On Foucault and neoliberalism, see Mitchell Dean, "Foucault must not be defended," *History and Theory,* 54 (2015), 389–403, and Andrew Dilts, "From 'entrepreneur of the self' to 'care of the self': Neo-liberal governmentality and Foucault's ethics," *Foucault Studies,* 12 (2011), 130–146. Foucault's work on biopower and biopolitics was only initial within his lifetime and can be mainly found at the end of the first volume of *The History of Sexuality.* For a more detailed discussion and a sense of how an entire subfield emerged out of these initial, if potent, reflections, see Timothy Campbell and Adam Sitze, eds., *Biopolitics: A Reader* (Duke University Press, 2013).

[113] Clements, "Foucault's Christianities," 28.

[114] Clements, *Sites of the Ascetic Self,* 179–180. At stake in this question, as feminist philosopher Cressida Heyes observes, is to what extent Foucault imagines this work of self-making to be a form of freedom and sovereignty, and to what extent he imagines this work to be always fraught, constrained by norms. Heyes's work on Foucault and self-transformation finds him in the latter territory, advocating not for an entrepreneurial self, allied with social norms, but rather for an unfinished project of self-stylization – one with no clear teleology. Self-transformation's best hopes are its uncertain conclusions. See Cressida Heyes, *Anaesthetics of Existence: Essays about Experience on the Edge* (Duke University Press, 2020) and Heyes, *Self-Transformations: Foucault, Ethics, and Normalized Bodies* (Oxford University Press, 2007).

[115] Clements, *Sites of the Ascetic Self,* 180–181.

she writes, "can be viewed as a radical attempt to construct a self whose every single quotidian activity, from sneezing to shoe-lacing, is shaped and reflected upon through the prism of commitment to the law, and thus as shaping a mode of living that entails incessant self-scrutiny and striving for self-perfection."[116] Within an extensive discussion of rabbinic legal concerns with purity, one that takes cues from Mary Douglas's work in *Purity and Danger*, Balberg recasts rabbinic legislation as constituting its own distinct form of the Greco-Roman self-stylization that Foucault describes, one which hinges on ritual performance. While Balberg is more interested in the way the rabbis are crafting a new understanding of Jewish subjectivity, one tightly allied to purity, one could also ask of her work how understanding this iteration of ethical self-formation might re-craft Foucault's history, which does not take Jewish sources into account.

In any case, it is worth noticing that Foucault's most controversial and politically ambivalent work, and his work most squarely centered on individuals (rather than institutions), is what has most captured the attention of studies of religion in late antiquity. One striking counterexample is Beth Berkowitz's *Execution and Invention: Death Penalty Discourse in Early Rabbinic and Christian Cultures*, which works with Foucault's *Discipline and Punish*. Berkowitz's book is in some ways participating in the larger tendency in the field to describe Jewish and Christian identity construction or the "invention" of Christianity and Judaism. But Berkowitz also draws from Foucault's recognitions that punishment is deeply social, epistemological, and symptomatic of power relations.[117] While rabbinic discourses about punishment and execution might have appeared less spectacularly horrifying than Roman ones, Berkowitz takes up Foucault's observations that "what looks like reform can still be understood as a technology of power." For the rabbis, then, death penalty discourse – and it was, most of the time largely discourse rather than practice – was about instantiating rabbinic authority to perform justice in the chaotic period after the first Jewish war, with unequivocal subjection under Rome. She writes, "I take issue with the assumption that because the rabbinic death penalty was likely never practiced, it was not a part of 'real' history."[118]

There have additionally been Foucauldian-inflected meta-reflections on the field itself as disciplinary knowledge-production, subject formation, and consolidation of norms and normative desires. These speak to the more

---

[116] Mira Balberg, *Purity, Body, and Self in Early Rabbinic Literature* (University of California Press, 2014), 11.

[117] Deth Berkowitz, *Execution and Invention: Death Penalty Discourse in Early Rabbinic and Christian Culture* (Oxford University Press, 2006), 8.

[118] Berkowitz, *Execution and Invention*, 18.

destabilizing dimensions of Foucault's work. Alexis Waller, for instance, has written about how discourses of forgery and/or authenticity in studies of early Christian texts are a "taxonomic project" that regulate and discipline desires in the writing of history, allowing and disallowing various forms of relations between scholars and their objects of study.[119] Compatibly, with a less overt relationship to Foucault, Greg Given writes a history of the collection of practices and dispositions that came to be recognized as "critical" in the nineteenth century as they emerged with and through the production of an "authentic" corpus of writings attributed to Ignatius of Antioch.[120]

The question posed in both of these intellectual projects is: how do disciplinary practices condition what we want out of history? In some ways, Foucault's work is a good temperature gauge for this very question. Foucault's work is so substantial and his influence so massive that he sometimes lives on simply as a (or even *the*) figure for "theory" itself. He is part of a set of citational practices that signal sophistication or "edginess." Because of the vastness of his work and influence, however, the particular *ways* in which "Foucault" appears tell us much about how we have been conditioned to engage: always first with a cautious investment in historical detail, even as Foucault was always trying to loosen us away from what we know to the much more unnerving investigation of how we have come to know it.

Foucault obviously funds the field in many implicit and explicit ways. We might also ask how Foucault's interest in late ancient Christianity funds his theorizing. Foucault, like Brown, is interested in late ancient Christianity as a period of change, even while the associated changes were often vague. As Averil Cameron notes, Foucault's history of sexuality is "explicitly associated with the history of Christianization; change from public morality to private, internalized virtue can even be said to 'explain' the triumph of Christianity."[121]

Foucault vacillated on his explanations of the changes of this period, as Elizabeth Castelli and Daniel Boyarin notice. On the one hand, Foucault describes a "near absolute" shift from the control of the will and the penetrative model of sexuality in classical Greek thought to the anxious eradication of desire in Christian asceticism (Foucault especially discussed John Cassian). On the other hand, Foucault also writes that "[I]t hardly makes any sense to talk about a 'Christian sexual ethic.' . . . The coming of Christianity, considered as

[119] Alexis Waller, "Forgeries of desire: The erotics of authenticity in New Testament historiography." Doctoral dissertation. Harvard Divinity School. 2021.

[120] J. Gregory Given, "Ignatius of Antioch and the historiography of early Christianity." Doctoral dissertation. Harvard University. 2019.

[121] Averil Cameron, "Redrawing the map: Early Christian territory after Foucault," *Journal of Roman Studies*, 76 (1986), 266–271.

a massive rupture with earlier moralities and the dominant introduction of a quite different one, is barely noticeable. As P. Brown says, in speaking of Christianity as part of our reading of the giant mass of antiquity, the topography of the parting of the waters is hard to pin down."[122]

For Foucault, then, Christianization was a parable about the rise of new forms of power, but it was also an extended example of the disruptions and disjunctures of history – his genealogical and archaeological approach.[123] As such, the tension between what is distinctive about the Christian self and its historical continuities (or its legibility in the context of the ancient world) was also perhaps a test of the limits of genealogies of history. What constitutes a "break"? How should one distinguish epistemologically between a "break" and a *sui generis* invention?

Of course, as Foucault's citation of Brown intimates, practically Brown's entire ouvre tries to name with tender specificity what exactly late antiquity *is*, what justifies it as a period, and what makes it compelling. Another way to understand Brown and Foucault's struggle with Christianization and late antiquity as a period is to understand it as a struggle with the *uniqueness* of Christianity, Christianity as substance and event. That is, they were in a struggle with Christian exceptionalism. Brown and Foucault, in the end, seem to substantiate exceptionalist narratives: their mutual influence fortifies a sense of a distinctly constituted Christian self that has a surprising amount of coherence. That two European men, themselves steeped in Christian culture and European (Christian) imperialism, might have something invested in proving the extraordinariness and coherence of an imperial Christianity is not so surprising, even if the political implications of these exceptionalist subtleties differ.[124] For Brown, the Christian empire and its propagators become sites of creativity, innovation, and even of sympathy. For Foucault, they become a launch point for both an art of living, and the most insidious forms of power and control.

A theory of Christianization does not need to substantiate Christian uniqueness, though. Two studies, both published in 2008, show how descriptions and theories of Christianization can actually highlight the mundanity of Christianization and Christian identity. The first (discussed further in Section 3) is Jeremy Schott's *Christianity, Empire, and the Making of Religion in Late Antiquity*. For Schott, the question of how the Roman empire became Christian

---

[122] Castelli and Boyarin, "Introduction," 362–363.

[123] Foucault's "archaeology of knowledge" refers to a critical approach to history, the object of which is to understand the production of historically specific truths and the implicit rules by which the production of truth is governed. See *The Order of Things: An Archaeology of the Human Sciences* (New York: Random House, 1970).

[124] Thanks to Andrew Jacobs for pointing this out.

assumes Christianity and empire are invariable entities that only join in late antiquity. As an alternative, Schott lays out the ways Christian discourses and imperial discourses were mutually constituting and facilitated, in part, by the growing centrality of "religion" for understanding belonging.[125] It seems that, for Schott, Christianization is only circumstantially a distinct collective rhetorical and social process: the functions of empire as population naming and management remained continuous.[126] Another way to put it is that the Christian empire is no strange animal or unique accomplishment as much as it is a parable of empire's continual remaking of itself.

The second study, Mike Chin's *Grammar and Christianity in the Late Roman World*, suggests Christian identity and the notion of "classical" culture were each produced in and through the unromantic daily discipline of grammatical work. Grammatical education fragments and reorganizes texts and in the process reorganizes time and subjectivity. That is, grammatical education allows its practitioners to envision themselves as part of an entity in relationship to a vaunted past. Christianization, for Chin, is not an event, but rather a narrative imagination accomplished only in the accretions and slow labors of textual parsing.[127] Understanding identity as "contingent temporal artifacts," Chin moves away from models of "conversion and affiliation" that fund most studies of Christianization in the Roman empire.[128] Chin writes:

> Removing Christianization from the category of historical events and placing it within the category of contingent identifying narratives, however, does not mean that Christianization cannot be studied historically, for history is obviously no stranger to narrative ... Rather than asking how or why Augustine became Christian, we might ask at what points, and under what conditions, might late ancient readers or writers have recognized a narrative or text as having Christianizing effects? (172)

I want to return to Brown's conceit at the beginning of *The Making of Late Antiquity* that we might wake up with surprise to this era, as well as to his sense, as described in *Body and Society*, of Christian late antiquity's strangeness. While underground exceptionalisms may guide Brown's picture of history, there is also something more than exceptionalism. Strangeness does not necessarily or always mean extraordinariness, as his quotidian examples of swimmers in California and Egypt suggest. Further, the strangeness of late antiquity is not

---

[125] Jeremy Schott, *Christianity, Empire, and the Making of Religion in Late Antiquity* (University of Pennsylvania Press, 2008).

[126] Schott, *Christianity, Empire, and the Making of Religion in Late Antiquity*, 167.

[127] Catherine Michael Chin, *Grammar and Christianity in the Late Roman World* (University of Pennsylvania Press, 2008). Chin's approach is largely poststructuralist in orientation, given its emphasis on language and subject formation.

[128] Chin, *Grammar*, 173.

only a quality of the period; it is also implied to be the result of a mode of defamiliarizing perception. It is to approach historical actors and phenomena with an eye toward their sympathetic quirkiness and with a sense of human companionability and wonder, in order to conjecture with curiosity about their experiences and motivations. Notably, this sense of wonder is transmitted most through Brown's rhapsodic prose.

Such a conjectural and lyrical style, such a desire to imaginatively live *inside* the late ancient world and its unfamiliar logics, has been heightened, sharpened in the work of other scholars. Take, for example, Patricia Cox Miller's dark and delicate pictures of late antiquity and her imagistic or sometimes musical interjections in the middle of her scholarly prose: "What kind of self emerges in the light of the transparent sphere?" she writes of Plotinus.[129] She plunges the reader into the sensibilities of the period. She joins late ancient writers in their imaginations as much as she describes them. So too we find affinity in Virginia Burrus's writing, with her lilting prose and forays into poetry combined with, on many occasions, genuine attachment and identification with late ancient figures.[130] Many of these figures Burrus reads through analytics of queerness, which has its own defamiliarizing and sympathetic effect, removing saints and ascetics from their stark and hardened positions in a normatively constructed Christian history.[131] We can likewise see some of these same long-running impulses in Michael Motia's essay, "Bluets of Late Antiquity: Polychromy and Christian Mysticism," which is not just a study of aesthetics but an almost elegaic experience of color: a historical riff on Maggie Nelson's poetic and philosophical reflection on the color blue.[132]

Lyricism in the study of late antiquity has quietly taken on the status of a method: a way of lavishing almost loving attention onto texts or figures, to make contact differently with history, and to do so by entering into the language and images and moods of late antiquity *as experience*, to get a little lost there.[133] Not incidentally, this lyrical "method" does have, as Miller herself has pointed

---

[129] Patricia Cox Miller, *The Corporeal Imagination: Signifying the Holy in Late Ancient Christianity* (University of Pennsylvania Press, 2009), 27.

[130] See, for example, Burrus, "Macrina's tattoo," *Journal of Medieval and Early Modern Studies*, 33 (2003), 403–417, and Burrus's personal reflections in the preface to *Saving Shame*, entitled "My shame," ix–xii.

[131] Michael Motia, "Bluets of late antiquity: Polychromy and Christian mysticism," *Studies in Late Antiquity*, 6(2022), 335–369.

[132] Maggie Nelson, *Bluets* (Wave Books, 2009).

[133] On the porousness of history and touches across time as expressed in queer historiography, see Carolyn Dinshaw, *Getting Medieval: Sexualities and Communities, Pre- and Postmodern* (Duke University Press, 1999) and Carla Freccero, *Queer/Early/Modern* (Duke University Press, 2006).

out, some interesting compatibility with the not insignificant amount of late ancient philosophizing on language and image.[134]

This quality of beautiful strangeness, which is also a mode of perception, has been theorized at some length in Mike Chin's widely admired essay, "Marvelous Things Heard: On Finding Historical Radiance." While Chin makes no mention of Brown, the essay seems to reverberate with or to channel Brown's sensibilities with its encouragement toward wonder at the alterity of the ancient world, its dedication to "the weirdness of history," its emphasis on empathy without domestication. Going beyond Brown, and wanting something deeper than a heightened aesthetic attention, Chin accords a moral importance to this posture of wonder that preserves history's weirdness: "the moral immediacy of encounter with what is not like us."[135] Radiance can *only* be encountered, it cannot be made, and that encounter is often unsettling. He continues:

> In strange worlds, we are weightless and strange ourselves. That is our moral beginning. Yet in return for looking for the strange, and allowing ourselves to be eclipsed by it, we are also allowed to find delight in stories of copper that grows from the ground, mice that collect gold or eat iron, or even the bewildering prospect of golden hemorrhoids as sacrificial offerings. (490)

It could be that after the loosened grip of triumphalist awe directed at Constantinian Christianity, and the Gibbons-esque moralizing about decay, a late antiquity that is imperfect but soaked in a beautiful strangeness can act as a balm. The late ancient world is neither ruined nor exceptional in these readings. These readings also eschew appeals to any overt or clear relationship to the present. That is, their defamiliarization requires no genealogical method. It rather requires an aesthetic one: the late ancient world is complexly, curiously, sensibly *different*. The "moral" dimension of this posture, however, as Chin notes, is not just a matter of encountering other worlds in all their offbeat glory. It is a matter of how those dizzying encounters relativize and disorient us from the normalities of our own.

3 Colonial Histories and the Vexations of the Global

> There is no one among us who, during the course of these difficult years, each day more tragic than the last, has not perceived like a flash of lightning piercing the apocalyptic night, the radical contingency of the earthly city. And this experience, like the sack of Rome by the Visigoths of Alaric for the contemporaries of

---

[134] Patricia Cox Miller, *The Poetry of Thought in Late Antiquity: Essays in Imagination and Religion* (Routledge, 2001).

[135] Catherine Michael Chin, "Marvelous things heard: On finding historical radiance," *Massachusetts Review*, 58 (2017), 478–491, at 490.

Augustine, has for those who lived it, a permanent value. It is our role, as witnesses, to recall it again when everything seems briefly to be working out for us and those around us; it is up to us to deepen it and draw the lesson from it.

(Henri-Irénée Marrou, Theologie de l'histoire, *1968, my translation)*

Henri-Irénée Marrou was one of the early scholars questioning Edward Gibbons's description of the late Roman empire as a period of decadence and decline. Writing from France in the early and mid-twentieth century, he was struggling with how to reckon with history writ large. Grappling with the aspirations of modernism, the annihilations of war, and, specifically, French colonialism in Algeria, Marrou was both writing a history of the later Roman period – particularly through Augustine of Hippo, who hailed from what is now Algeria – and philosophizing on history more generally.[136] Augustine was not just a figure to be rethought in the context of what would soon be known broadly as "late antiquity," but offered an interpretive key for bridging the gap between the empty and disillusioning eventfulness of the early twentieth century and a sense of existential significance. That is, Marrou does not just write about Augustine. He joins Augustine in postulating about the meaning of history.

As Thomas Hunt and others have chronicled, the history and archaeology of Roman North Africa was over this period of time "a process of integrating the material remnants of the Roman past into the time and space of the French empire."[137] Marrou's career was marked by vocal discontent with French colonialism generally and the long-term violence done to Algeria specifically. Yet this was not always up front in Marrou's scholarship on late antiquity.[138] Rather, as Hunt shows, while Marrou had profound worries about the heaviness of being implicated in France's exploitation and war-making, and what his work in late antiquity meant as a result, Marrou metabolizes these worries in his scholarship with something of a light touch.

In two separate articles, Hunt argues for a fuller consideration of mid-twentieth-century scholarship on late antiquity and its extensive colonial entanglements. He argues that, beyond Marrou and his disaffection, much of the scholarship on patristics in this period in France was defined by colonialism – not only by the

---

[136] See Henri-Irénée Marrou (under the pseudonym Henri Davenson), *Fondemonts d'une culture Chretienne* (Librairie Bloud and Gay, 1934) and *Saint Augustin et la fin de la culture antique, avec Retractatio* (De Boccard, 1949).

[137] Thomas Hunt, "Imperial collapse and Christianization in patristic scholarship during the final decades of colonial Algeria, 1930–1962," *Journal of Early Christian Studies*, 29 (2021), 272. Hunt cites Bonnie Effros's important book, *Incidental Archaeologists: French Officers and the Rediscovery of Roman North Africa* (Cornell University Press, 2018).

[138] Thomas Hunt, "Imperial collapse and Christianization," 286. See Marrou's article in the French newspaper *Le Monde*, in which he vocally objects to the unfolding of the war in Algeria and for which, Hunt recounts, Marrou's apartment was raided by the French police. Marrou, "France, ma patrie," *Le Monde*, April 5, 1956.

experience of political events, but also "by models of human difference, time, and space that grew from the imperial imaginary of the French Republic."[139] Hunt urges the field to take stock of the ways the study of late ancient Christianity has facilitated colonial projects, including through the matrices of geography and periodization.

Scholarship since Marrou has, for the most part, not gotten more overt or direct about its own reckonings with and within contemporary colonial systems and knowledge projects. Indeed, in many cases, the scholars who have begun to think about ancient history more consciously in the wake of the vast and ongoing project of (neo)colonialism, discussed in this section, have generally tread more lightly than Marrou in terms of claiming their politics. At the very same time, these scholars produce some of the most destabilizing work in the field. This perhaps has something to do with the inherent conservatisms of the now more clearly professionalized fields of ancient history and classics – where the study of religion in late antiquity tends to find itself situated (or rather where it finds itself *legitimated*).[140] To speak of "politics" is then perhaps to risk seeming too much like theology with its more openly subjective ruminations and its vested interests in contemporary meaning-making.

For example, let us return to Schott's *Christianity, Empire, and the Making of Religion in the Roman Empire*. Schott's book is nothing if not an extended historical case study on the rhetorical and discursive microfunctions of empire and the effects of their accumulation. Schott is explicit about his debt to postcolonial discourse analysis, but he anticipates critique for this debt, which draws from theories devised from modern empires to understand ancient ones. "Some scholars, however, have questioned the applicability of postcolonial theory to premodern contexts, contending that the discursive formations of nineteenth- and twentieth-century imperialism – especially the particular racial theories and economic systems employed by European colonialists – did not obtain in premodern contexts."[141] He notes another critique: "Some Roman historians, moreover, resist analogies between ancient Roman and modern imperialisms on the grounds that Rome had no systematic mercantile or capitalistic interest in her territories."[142] Countering such objections, he notes that not only has postcolonial theory been productively brought to other premodern

---

[139] Hunt, "Imperial collapse," 288. See also Thomas Hunt, "The influence of French colonial humanism on the study of late antiquity: Braudel, Marrou, Brown," *International Journal of Francophone Studies*, 21 (2019), 255–278.

[140] David Mattingly's scholarship is a counterpoint in that his work on imperialism in late antiquity is passionately interested. See Mattingly, *Imperialism, Power, and Identity: Experiencing the Roman Empire* (Princeton University Press, 2013).

[141] Schott, *Christianity, Empire, and the Making of Religion in Late Antiquity*, 10.

[142] Schott, *Christianity, Empire, and the Making of Religion in Late Antiquity*, 10.

societies but it also offers a "necessary corrective to studies of the Roman world that obscure or ignore the material consequences of domination."[143] Making his case in the plainest terms possible, Schott writes:

> Rome, after all, conquered and controlled territory and people, established colonies, and controlled its subjects via provincial bureaucracies. The Roman Empire was a diverse place but not an equal one. The right to rule was based on polarized differences between rulers and the ruled, between the metropolitan center and the provincial periphery. Consequently, establishing oneself or others as Greek, Roman, Egyptian or Jewish was not an academic exercise. (10)

Although this book was published in 2008, one still often needs to make a defense for applying "colonialism" to late ancient texts. In 2018, Carly Daniel-Hughes and I submitted an article on Tertullian to the *Journal of Early Christian Studies*.[144] A primary critique of one of the reviewers asked brusquely how it was possible to speak in colonial terms of late ancient North Africa – a Roman colony. These scenes of apology/defense of critiques of colonialism often arrive in the package of historical specificity. Their force, however, suggests and often effects a foreclosure of connection between ancient and contemporary forms of colonialism. To speak even analogically of modern empire is to have sacrificed your credentials as a historian. Of course, absenting connections of empire-making across time and space is part of how empire and colonialism refuse to be known. Lisa Lowe's *The Intimacies of Four Continents* approaches and theorizes this problem by connecting histories and historical archives that have often been forcefully separated, demonstrating how histories of liberalism converge with conditions of subjugation and exploitation.[145] Scholars of late antiquity have only had the most tentative opportunities to do the same. At the end of Schott's book, he writes about the utility of late ancient Christian apologetics in modernity and he offers pages of striking examples in which patristic material becomes the interpretive lens for representing non-European people, from European "discovery," to colonial administrators in Peru, to the classifications of "world religions."[146] The name of the final chapter is "Empire's Palimpsest" and the eviscerating takeaway is that "religion" has been deployed over time in the service of – and to hide – racializing schemas and other colonial relations. This is Schott's "epilogue."

---

[143] Schott, *Christianity, Empire, and the Making of Religion in Late Antiquity*, 10.

[144] Carly Daniel-Hughes and Maia Kotrosits, "Tertullian of Carthage and the fantasy life of power: On martyrs, Christians, and other attachments to juridical scenes," *Journal of Early Christian Studies*, 28 (2020), 1–31.

[145] Lisa Lowe, *The Intimacies of Four Continents* (Duke University Press, 2015).

[146] Schott, *Christianity, Empire, and the Making of Religion in Late Antiquity*, 170–175.

We might consider Schott's epilogue alongside Andrew Jacobs's work. Jacobs's body of scholarship represents the most sustained postcolonial recalibration of religion in late antiquity and, in sum, fashions an extensive history of the machinations of colonial difference that manifest in Christian late antiquity. Each of his books represents a case study in this history. His earliest book, *Remains of the Jews*, shows how Christian writings about Jews, as well as Christian imaginations of Jerusalem and the holy land, were part of an imperializing identity-craft. Christian writers used various rhetorical tactics to achieve this, including confining Jewishness to the past, creating prestigious and objectifying knowledge about Jewishness or Jews ("academic imperialism"), and fetishistically associating the holy land with sensual experience. Jacobs's introduction recounts his project's debt to "postcolonial criticism,"[147] specifically the work of Edward Said, Gayatri Spivak, and Homi Bhabha, who had become (and remain) canonical figures of postcolonial criticism and theory.[148] All of this work has a Foucauldian genealogy and is thoroughly part of the linguistic turn. Jacobs, however, also draws from a wider pool, for instance, Ranajit Guha, Robert Young, Mary Louise Pratt, and Ann McClintock, whose work on empire and colonialism has still not seen much interest in the field.[149]

Like Schott, Jacobs leans most on what is the fundamental, or at least the most recognizable, insight of this strand of postcolonial theory: that neither colonized nor colonizer (nor their respective cultures) remain intact or unchanged with colonial encounter. This is what Bhabha terms "hybridity."[150] Also like Schott, Jacobs understands colonial identities to be inherently unstable, to demand constant renegotiation and fortification, a process of continual rhetorical improvisation. Jacobs, however, additionally emphasizes that he is not painting a picture of

---

[147] Jacobs concertedly differentiates postcolonial criticism from postcolonial theory and postcolonial studies, the latter of which would indicate "an overarching explanatory narrative." *Remains of the Jew*, 7, note 23.

[148] See Jacobs, *Remains of the Jew*, 8–11. The classic texts include Homi Bhabha, *The Location of Culture* (Routledge, 1994); Edward Said, *Orientalism* (Pantheon, 1978) and *Culture and Imperialism* (Alfred A. Knopf, 1993); and Gayatri Chakravorty Spivak, "Can the subaltern speak?" in C. Nelson and L. Grossberg (eds.), *Marxism and the Interpretation of Culture*, (Macmillan, 1988). See also Spivak's *A Critique of Postcolonial Reason: Toward a History of the Vanishing Present* (Harvard University Press, 1999).

[149] For instance, see Ranajit Guha, "On some aspects of the historiography of colonial India," *Subaltern Studies*, 45 (1994), 86–91; Anne McClintock, *Imperial Leather: Race, Gender, and Sexuality in the Colonial Contest* (Routledge, 1995); Mary Louise Pratt, *Imperial Eyes: Travel Writing and Transculturation* (Routledge, 1992); Robert Young, *Colonial Desire: Hybridity in Theory, Culture, and Race* (Routledge, 1995).

[150] Hybridity hails from botany, in which plant hybridity, the emergence of a new plant species, was tied up in racialized fantasies of separating "pure" from "mixed" species. Bhabha redefines hybridity to disturb ideas of purity and to describe the emergence of colonial culture as *always* mixed, always in the process of change and translation.

uncontested domination of Christians over Jews: with any colonial act of territorialization comes new openings for resistance and interruption by those being disenfranchised, possibilities that plagued the Christian imagination. Jacobs writes:

> The colonialist fantasies of erasure, conquest, and appropriation cannot help but evoke their dreaded opposites: resistance, uprising, and colonial mimicry, those methods by which the objects of imperial authority reclaim some measure of power through those same cultural processes by which colonizer and colonized are dialectically constructed. (198)

Jacobs's other books excavate the history of imperializing difference in late antiquity from two considerably more quirky and oblique angles. *Christ Circumcised* considers how ancient Christians tried to unravel the perpetual knot Christian difference via the bodily sign of Jesus' foreskin or lack thereof.[151] Jacobs's book *Epiphanius of Cyprus* takes as its starting point and historical linchpin a figure often subject to eyerolls or dismissal by historians, and this figure just happens to be a connoisseur and master manager of difference in all of its engrossing and unresolved iterations. These books too are driven by postcolonial epistemologies – the former with more psychoanalytic intonations – and describe the imperial hunger to visually materialize, taxonomize, exaggerate, manage, and, of course, dominate others. But in the very end of *Epiphanius of Cyprus,* Jacobs pitches a line out past the period he has in these three books so fulsomely diagnosed. From the book's final paragraph:

> Epiphanius' late antiquity complicates our ideas about difference in society: in this late antiquity, a bishop achieves prominence by twisting the possibilities of difference into an opportunity for the performative exercise of power and control. To take Epiphanius seriously as a representative figure of late antiquity, a late antiquity in which (so often) we find shadows of our own cultural concerns, leads us to ask, to what extent does our own multicultural society make similarly twisted uses of "difference" in the public sphere? By marginalizing certain uncomfortable figures from our canonical field of late antiquity, what "problems and questions" of our own might we be refusing to bring to the forefront? (277)

It is a gentle prod with menacing ramifications. Let me express it a bit differently: if we look too hard at Epiphanius we might see in his exaggerated gestures and unsavory character the imperializing and manipulative heart of forms of seemingly benign multiculturalism and diversity politics that define our present. Although Jacobs does not go so far as to suggest it, we could stretch

---

[151] Jacobs, *Remains of the Jew*, 198.

his conclusion to imagine an alternative to Foucault's genealogy. Foucault finds in late ancient Christianity the structures and portents of later forms of disciplinary power and interiorized self-regulation. But we might find in Jacobs's work a picture of how the investments in and recapitulations of difference that intensified in Christian thought – to the point of sacralized obsession – reawaken in a different but no less defining dimension of neoliberalism: the constant proliferation, materialization, and organization of individual identities in relationship to state naming, recognition, and inclusion. What would it be like to draw those lines more directly?

In many cases, the most destabilizing possibilities of anti- and postcolonial critiques remain latent because this work has not yet been aggregated and integrated. It is also, however, because some of this work hovers between metaphorical and material applications of postcolonial critique. Take, for instance, Peter Mena's *Place and Identity in the Lives of Antony, Paul, and Mary of Egypt*, which plays with the possibilities of Gloria Anzaldúa's work as he reads Christian hagiography's imaginative landscape of the desert as a zone of contact and new subjectivity formation. That is, it is functioning in the same way as the borderlands/frontier described by Anzaldúa. While Mena refers to this Christian subjectivity as a "desert *mestizaje*,"[152] Mena is coy about whether this imagined borderlands has real ancient sociopolitical referents. Borderlands, for Mena, appear mostly as a metaphor, but it does not need to be. We could read Mena integratively with Walter Ward's *Mirage of the Saracen*, which primarily reads not hagiography, but the Sinai martyr narratives. Ward reveals how the Christian representation of indigenous nomadic peoples in the Sinai desert as violent and savage peoples smoothed the path for the monastic colonization of the area. The Sinai martyr narratives, for Ward, are best understood as fortifications and elaborations of Christian identity via the inverse image of the indigenous people they encountered. Echoing Jacobs's understanding of how the holy land functioned in Christian travel writing, and consonant with Mena, Ward considers the Sinai desert as borderlands through the work of Anzaldúa, and as a liminal place where colonial contact both presents a crisis of self-understanding and becomes the ground on which it is asserted.[153]

---

[152] Mena, *Place and Identity in the Lives of Antony, Paul, and Mary of Egypt*, 4. Compatibly, see Justo L. Gonzalez, *The Mestizo Augustine: A Theologian between Two Cultures* (Intervarsity Press, 2016).

[153] Walter Ward, *The Mirage of the Saracen: Christians and Nomads in the Sinai Peninsula in Late Antiquity* (University of California Press, 2014). Ward engages Bhabha and Spivak as well. See especially pages 8–12. Saracens are a perfect example of Spivak's "subalterns" for Ward.

We could add to this some of the work theorizing ethnicity and racialization.[154] As Schott argues, part of the work of "religion" as a marker of belonging has been, over time, to override and even efface ethnicity and race, even as "religion" can have racializing effects.[155] Gay Byron and Denise Buell have drawn attention specifically to how ethnicity and racializing logics were used to shape Christian self-understanding.[156] For Byron, Egyptians, Ethiopians, and black-skinned figures in Christian literature are part of "ethno-political rhetorics"; they are representations that have symbolic and polemical significance rather than referential value. Likewise for Buell, the "ethnic reasoning" used by ancient Christians still subtly preserves ethnicity as a metaphor for Christian belonging.[157] What if we took more seriously, even took as our foundation, forms of local and ethnic belonging ("of Carthage"; "of Antioch") that these figures seem to want to transcend with Christian belonging? In other words, it is easy to forget that these figures have histories and contexts and relationships to locations that are not secondary to their work and to their sense of the world just because they were more interested in talking, at least sometimes, about being Christian. It could very well be that these "other" forms of belonging are perhaps more pressing to them, if also more taken for granted, than any kind of Christian belonging.[158]

****

---

[154] While ethnicity and race tend to signify different things, mainly culture and biology, respectively, I hold the two terms together here (and in my other work) in order to gesture to the fact that culture and race have never been fully separable categories, albeit ones that construct difference in specific ways. Likewise, I use racialization to name the ways that race is indeed not a natural, biological category at all, but a process of naturalization of population production.

[155] Schott is obviously not alone in this. See especially Tomoko Masuzawa, *The Invention of World Religions: How European Universalism Was Preserved in the Language of Pluralism* (University of Chicago Press, 2005) and more recently, Geraldine Heng, *The Invention of Race in the European Middle Ages* (Cambridge University Press, 2018).

[156] Gay L. Byron, *Symbolic Blackness and Ethnic Difference in Early Christian Literature* (Routledge, 2002). Denise Buell, *Why This New Race? Ethnic Reasoning in Early Christianity* (Columbia University Press, 2005). See also Brakke, "Ethiopian demons."

[157] For a sampling of other work on Christianity and ethnicity and racialization, see Terrence Keel's *Divine Variations: How Christian Thought Became Racial Science* (Stanford University Press, 2018), which builds on Buell's work. See also Todd Berzon, *Classifying Christians: Ethnography, Heresiology, and the Limits of Knowledge in Late Antiquity* (University of California Press, 2021) and Aaron Johnson, *Ethnicity and Argumentation in Eusebius' Praeparatio Evangelica* (Oxford University Press, 2006). Matthew Chalmers's "Past Paul's Jewishness: The Bejaminite Paul in Epiphanius of Cyrus," *Harvard Theological Review*, 115 (2022), 309–330, significantly nuances and refines the terms for thinking Jewishness, ethnicity, and affiliation in late ancient Christian imaginations.

[158] See, for instance, Éric Rebillard, *Christians and Their Many Identities in Late Antiquity, North Africa, 200–450 CE* (Cornell University Press, 2017). Carly Daniel-Hughes and I have also proposed this. See, for example, Daniel-Hughes and Kotrosits, "Tertullian of Carthage and the fantasy life of power."

The long history of Christian imperialism and all it implies haunts the study of religion in late antiquity. Rightly so, since Christian imperialism is the defining feature of late antiquity. Appreciating how this hauntedness shapes the field is another question, however. For instance, while critique of dominant identity formation is obviously necessary, so much of the postcolonial work in the field has revolved around Christian identity (or Greek or Roman identity) as the endgame of drawing out the efficacies of texts and representations. This is perhaps linked to the poststructuralist bent of so much of this work. One great shortcoming of poststructuralist epistemologies, as Rey Chow shows, is the never-ending loop of self-referentiality – that is, every representation points back to the presiding entity – the one doing the representing.[159] The problem is that this does not leave much room for others without being "Others."

There have been circumnavigations of this tendency: *Jews, Christians, and the Roman Empire*, a volume coedited by Natalie B. Dorhmann and Annette Yoshiko Reed, is a collection of essays in which one overt goal is to understand Romanization through the minoritized and seemingly "outside" position of Jews – Jews within Roman provincial culture provide dynamic, specified instances of Christianization. Accounting for the experiences and effects of empire, including its reproduction, simply looks different when centralizing nondominant groups and positions. The sheer volume of extant Jewish literature from this period means there is an especially rich repository from which to draw. Sarit Kattan Gribetz's *Time and Difference in Rabbinic Judaism*, for instance, offers an enthralling and almost phenomenological account of the ways Jewish belonging worked itself out in relationship to normativizing imperial clocks, calendars, and rhythms.[160] Her book is a meticulous illustration of how the epistemics of colonization are lived and opposed in ways that are daily, corporeal, and corporate.

Sara Ronis's work on the Babylonian Talmud too offers a different picture of lived colonial entanglements. In "Imagining the Other: The Magical Arab in Rabbinic Literature," Ronis argues that the rabbis employ stereotypical tropes of Arabs as exotic and mystical guides, purveyors of special wisdom, in a way that parallels the modern film trope of the "magical negro."[161] This stereotyping was of course common across the ancient world, a theme and variation on the "wise barbarian." Christian literature had its own depictions of Arabs in this

---

[159] Chow, *The Age of the World Target*.

[160] Sarit Kattan Gribetz, *Time and Difference in Rabbinic Judaism* (Princeton University Press, 2020).

[161] Sara Ronis, "Imagining the other: The magical Arab in rabbinic literature," *Prooftexts*, 29 (2021), 1–28. As Ronis notes, while apparently a more "positive" stereotype, the magical other is always a dehumanizing form of subordination and abstraction.

vein. What Ronis notices is the way that the figure of the magical Arab is not simply the repetition of an age-old trope of the wise foreigner. This trope works specifically within rabbinic literature to imagine a world "with the rabbis themselves at the geographic, cultural, and religious center."[162] This is, she notes, not the world in which the rabbis lived, with only tentative security under the Sasanians. Rather than attempting to make of Arab figures uncivilized objects of conversion (as Christians did), however, the rabbis used these figures to negotiate the globalization of the era. "Globalization is not an invention of the modern world," Ronis writes.[163]

Also compatible with Dorhman and Reed's goals is David Frankfurter's *Christianizing Egypt*, in which he pushes back on the widespread association of Christianity with an identity. He does so in order to tell more complex and local stories about the increased movement and production of Christianity in late antiquity. Quite apart from the aforementioned discursive analyses of Christianization, Frankfurter's approach is social and material. Frankfurter sets aside some of the darlings of postcolonial theory: Bhabha's hybridity and Spivak's question, "Can the subaltern speak?" For Frankfurter, there was no single relationship to Christianity in Egypt. Each of his illustrations (which include shrines and oracles, amulets and festivals) suggests intricate pushes and pulls between, and even artful arrangements of, Christian and traditional religion. He describes this as *"indigenous agency* in the development of meaning, and sometimes even the assertion of native culture within or against the new religious discourse."[164] He chooses to revive the once-abandoned category of "syncretism" over and against Bhabha's hybridity, though he carefully defines syncretism as *bricolage* and acknowledges that individual traditions are always already a concoction of elements. Syncretism "must be understood as an experimental assemblage, not a fixed and harmonious melding of ideas."[165]

Likewise more scholars have recently focused on the ways the Roman empire and Christianity in this period were not isolated and self-contained (and therefore exceptional or self-generated) phenomena, tracing texts and figures across geographical, sociopolitical, and religious boundaries.[166] Stephen Shoemaker's *The Apocalypse of Empire* collects instances of eschatological imaginations in Christianity, Judaism, Zoroastrianism, and early Islam to theorize apocalypticism

---

[162] Ronis, "Imagining the other," 20.   [163] Ronis, "Imagining the other," 1.

[164] David Frankfurter, *Christianizing Egypt: Syncretism and Local Worlds in Late Antiquity* (Princeton University Press, 2018), 17.

[165] Frankfurter, *Christianizing Egypt*, 17.

[166] In addition to those I name here, see, for instance, Greg Fisher, *Between Empires: Arabs, Romans, and Sasanians in Late Antiquity* (Oxford University Press, 2011), and Kyle Smith, *Constantine and the Captive Christians of Persia: Martyrdom and Religious Identity in Late Antiquity* (University of California Press, 2016).

as a shared and common parlance in this period.[167] So too Michael Pregill has drawn from biblical scholarship treating scripture as process (scripturalization) to follow the story of the golden calf in Jewish, Christian, and early Islamic textual traditions, demonstrating how reworkings of the story served the purposes of collective self-definition.[168]

It is not that dominant identity formation is an unimportant consideration at all. It is rather an issue of what is precluded in dominant identity-making as a field-wide habit of analysis. As this work I have just summarized shows, one thing that is sidelined by the focus on dominant identity construction is complex and local social histories that might bear out colonization as producing multifaceted and idiosyncratic sets of experiences. It can also sideline fuller descriptions of institutions and structures, or even of psychic life beyond "identity." We might, in other words, miss different epistemologies for historiography.

So too the ascendancy and popularization of postcolonial critique in the poststructuralist tradition regularly gives the impression that this is the sum total of postcolonial critique (even decades after Spivak, Bhabha, and Said wrote their most influential books). While one could hardly blame Spivak, Bhabha, or Said for coming up with concepts and questions that took on so much traction, the concepts and questions have been replicated so often that they very easily become abstracted from their deep contexts. This is also fast becoming the case with Christina Sharpe's "wake work" and Saidiya Hartman's "critical fabulation," which are appearing now with regularity in publications and conference papers over the past handful of years.[169] What happens to these living concepts, what gets done to them, when they become "hot"?[170] What

---

[167] Stephen Shoemaker, *The Apocalypse of Empire: Imperial Eschatology in Late Antiquity and Early Islam* (University of Pennsylvania Press, 2018).

[168] Michael E. Pregill, *The Golden Calf between Bible and Qur'an: Scripture, Polemic, and Exegesis from Late Antiquity to Islam* (Oxford University Press, 2020). Pregill draws from Vincent Wimbush and Jacqueline Hidalgo's respective work on scripturalizing.

[169] Christina Sharpe, *In the Wake: On Blackness and Being* (Duke University Press, 2016) and Saidiya Hartman, "Venus in two acts," *Small Axe*, 26 (2008), 1–14, and *Wayward Lives, Beautiful Experiments: Intimate Histories of Social Upheaval* (W. W. and Norton and Company, 2019). For examples of scholars drawing on Hartman, see Laura Nasrallah, "The work of nails: Religion, Mediterranean antiquity, and contemporary Black art," *Journal of the American Academy of Religion* (2022), Candida Moss, "Between the lines: Looking for contributions of enslaved literate laborers in a second-century text (P.Berol. 11632)," *Studies in Late Antiquity*, 5 (2021), 432–452, and David Maldonado Rivera, "Method, ethics, and historiography: A late ancient Caribbean in the temporalities of empire," *Ancient Jew Review*, January 25, 2022. More discussion of Maldonado Rivera's piece follows. For examples of scholars drawing on Sharpe, see Kotrosits, *The Lives of Objects*, chapter 3, and Laura Nasrallah, "*Christemporos*: Christ and the market in early Christian texts," *Biblical Interpretation*, 30 (2021), 509–537.

[170] Critical fabulation, for instance, is part of a genealogy in Black feminist studies that is important to keep in mind as it gets transported into other contexts. The embracing of fiction in critical fabulation also implies a *style of writing* that has been left behind (so far) as the concept moved

happens in their repetitions over time – when theoretical experiments become calcified into a "method"? Or, more troublingly, when is transporting an idea into your own context extending or renewing the life of that concept, and when is it simply a consumption and commodification of creativity?

I also wonder how the field would be different if other concepts had taken flight, or if they eventually do, or if the interlocutors on colonialism were more various: for a start, we might look to Suzanne Césaire on epistemological resistance via aesthetics, or C. L. R. James and Marxist accounts of resistance and de- or recentered histories, Audra Simpson on the intricacies of governance and political refusal, or Ariella Azoulay on imperial managements of the past.[171]

So many of the case studies offered in the postcolonial theoretical literature from which scholars of religion in late antiquity draw are from the height of European modernity. These are, of course, very rich and detailed case studies. But we might consider this: in the early 2000s, just as this canon of postcolonial theory was beginning to hit the field in the United States, the United States was the beating heart of neocolonialism on the world stage. The September 11th terrorist attacks and the war on terror (George W. Bush's "accidental" description of which was a "crusade"), state-sanctioned torture and the ramping up of new forms of nationalism were unfolding before our eyes at the very same moment many of us were learning about the finer points of colonial administration in the Dutch East Indies. At about that same time (2002), Israel began Operation Defensive Shield with its incursion into the West Bank, with thousands of Palestinians dead or injured and even more detained.

These two contexts alone have redirected the course of theorizing on colonialism, especially through the influential work of Jasbir Puar. Puar's 2007 book *Terrorist Assemblages* outlines the way the politics and statecraft emanating from 9/11 crystallized a particular set of social and structural formations, in which some queer subjects are aligned with national, biopolitical, and military projects in the name of progress and inclusion (homonationalism), at the expense of queerly racialized populations or populations figured outside of

---

into this field. On critical fabulation as related to the landmark work of Darlene Clark Hine, see Jennifer Nash, "Black feminine enigmas, or notes on the politics of black feminist theory," *Signs*, 45 (2020), 519–523. As Nash notes, one key dimension of Hartman's critical fabulation is a "critical interrogation of the feelings – desire, sorrow, loss, to name just a few – that historians bring to the archive" (521). Curiously, this too has been left behind as the concept moved into this field.

[171] For instance, see Suzanne Césaire, *The Great Camouflage: Writings of Dissent (1941–1945)*, ed. Daniel Mamin (Wesleyan University Press, 2012), Keith L. Walker, *The Black Jacobins: Toussaint L'Ouverture and the San Domingo Revolution*, trans. C. L. R. James (Secker and Warburg, 1938), Audra Simpson, *Mohawk Interruptus: Political Life across Borders of Settler States* (Duke University Press, 2014), Ariella Azoulay, *Potential History: Unlearning Imperialism* (Verso, 2019).

national and imperial borders.[172] Since this book's publication, queer theory has had a full and extensive reckoning with the limits of thinking queerness as or through resistance or subversion, and gender or sexuality as categories that function analogically to race. As the *SocialText* issue "Left of Queer" reveals, queerness has been institutionalized and nationalized, and it has trajectories beyond both sexuality and identity. So queer theory has begun reformulating itself as "subjectless critique."[173] A number of scholars in that issue – Marquis Bey, Aren Aizura, Jodi A. Byrd – theorize specifically how gender and sexuality are formed, made available, and produced within colonial and racializing schemas.

Puar's more recent book, *The Right to Maim*, outlines how neoliberal rights discourses around disability disguise the state management of populations through debility – in other words, through conditions of debilitation. To say it differently, the notion of disability as an identity that demands recognition and rights is marked by the centrality of whiteness, normativizing definitions of what disability is or is not, and a desire for state inclusion and flourishing that is not available for the vast majority of disabled people across the globe.[174] Policing and incarceration debilitates, labor exploitation debilitates, war debilitates. Puar coined the phrase "crip nationalism" to describe how "[t]he biopolitical distribution between disability as an exceptional accident or misfortune, and the proliferation of debilitation as war, as imperialism, as durational death, is largely maintained through disability rights frameworks."[175] Israel's militarized occupation of Palestine is her crowning illustration of the biopolitics of debility as population control.

Puar's work and the vast body of compatible work in cultural studies suggests that we should not be reading disability, gender, and sexuality as analytically separable, or even quite "intersecting."[176] Rather imperialism, colonialism, and racialization form the basis for our relationship to these other terms. Some of the scholarship in late antiquity studies has already laid the groundwork for this shift. Strikingly, Julia Watts Belser's *Rabbinic Tales of Destruction* combines analytics of sex, gender, and disability under the rubric of rabbinic responses to

[172] Jasbir K. Puar, *Terrorist Assemblages: Homonationalism in Queer Times* (Duke University Press, 2007).

[173] David L. Eng and Jasbir K. Puar, "Introduction in 'Left of queer,'" *Social Text*, 145 (2020), 1–23.

[174] Jasbir K. Puar, *The Right to Maim: Debility, Capacity, Disability* (Duke University Press, 2017), xix.

[175] Puar, *The Right to Maim*, 66.

[176] On the history, complex afterlives, and limits of intersectional models, see Jennifer Nash, *Black Feminism Reimagined: After Intersectionality* (Duke University Press, 2018) and Puar, *Terrorist Assemblages*, 212–213, as well as Puar's interview with Oishik Sircar, *Humanity*, 11.3 (2021).

Roman domination.[177] So too Gwynn Kessler's *Conceiving Israel* charts how, in rabbinic literature, the reproduction of peoplehood is configured in and through the (imagined) contents of the womb.[178]

Likewise a handful of studies in the field have already approached gender and sexuality as occurring within and consequent to colonialism and racialization. Susanna Drake's *Slandering the Jew*, for example, as well as Peter Mena's chapter on the Life of Mary of Egypt, which reads Mary's queer eroticism as an outgrowth of her life as a desert *mestiza*.[179] Earliest among these, and published in the same year, are Jennifer Knust's *Abandoned to Lust*, which drew from work in postcolonial studies and described moralizing sexual invective in the context of broader sociopolitical power relations, and Virginia Burrus's reading of virginity in some ancient novels as a symptom of cultural ambivalence.[180] Most thoroughly indebted to Puar and colleagues, and consonant with her hopes in "Mary Magdalene in the Fantasy Echo" to bring feminist historiography into a soft reckoning with itself, Carly Daniel-Hughes rereads Tertullian's treatises on women's dress – thoroughly critiqued by white feminist scholarship, including her own – as, at heart, about colonial anxieties, rather than simply patriarchal policing.[181]

I do not at all wish to limit or define the field's context for colonialism to Israeli occupation of Palestine and the war on terror. The contexts far exceed these. These contexts are old, myriad, constant, and evolving. A couple of questions we might also consider, however, inspired by Marrou, whose own colonial and global vexations were at the front of his mind, if not always on the surface of his work: What if this deep colonial morass we currently inhabit is not a source of comparison for late antiquity, with some fortunate parallels and some unfortunate limits, each to be carefully posed and parsed? What if we take

---

[177] Julia Watts Belser, *Rabbinic Tales of Destruction: Gender, Sex, and Disability in the Ruins of Jerusalem* (Oxford University Press, 2017). While there is a growing body of literature on disability and medicine with respect to religion in late antiquity, this literature has not generally met up with the vast body of literature in cultural studies theorizing disability, impairment, and debility.

[178] Gwynn Kessler, *Conceiving Israel: The Fetus in Rabbinic Narratives* (University of Pennsylvania Press, 2009).

[179] Mena, *Place and Identity*, 85–114.

[180] Jennifer Knust, *Abandoned to Lust: Sexual Slander and Ancient Christianity* (Columbia University Press, 2005). Virginia Burrus, "Mimicking virgins: Colonial ambivalence and the ancient romance," *Arethusa*, 38 (2005), 49–88.

[181] Carly Daniel-Hughes, "Adornments of empire: Feminine subjectivity and Roman colonial life in Tertullian of Carthage." Delivered at the 12th Enoch Nangeroni Meeting, "Constructions of Gender in Late Antiquity." Inspired by her paper and my conversations with Daniel-Hughes, I have suggested reconsidering gender as an object of study within ethnographic and medicalizing (pathologizing) imaginations in both antiquity and modernity. See Maia Kotrosits, "The ethnography of gender: Reconsidering gender as an object of analysis," *Studies in Late Antiquity* issue 7.1 (2023).

this morass to be the history into which late ancient literature flares and unfolds? We are *in* long histories of colonialism, not living in their aftermath. The information is before us, under our feet, and we live it every day. The ancient figures we study are in these long histories too.

Similar questions are posed by David Maldonado Rivera's brief but crucial reflection on method, ethics, and historiography, "A Late Ancient Caribbean in the Temporalities of Empire." He launches from an example of Catholic Church property disputes in Puerto Rico at the turn of the twentieth century. In this context, the Catholic Church legally retained expropriated property via juridical reasoning that placed the Catholic Church in Puerto Rico in a continuous line with Constantine, thereby instantiating "the church" as a transhistorical imperial entity. This legal logic thereby "turned Puerto Rico into one of the outermost and unlikeliest of territories of a Transatlantic Roman Empire, an eruption of late antiquity into the so-called American Century."[182] Maldonado Rivera notices how critical the organization of time as "linear, unavoidable sentence" is to the ongoing force of colonialism. To counter this colonial temporality, he suggests that historians "cultivate a 'diasporic consciousness' by thinking a historical commons as a tentative connection to the fragments of history rather than the irrefutable certainties of cosmopolitan linear universality."[183]

The chain of time is long, convoluted, ephemeral. That Maldonado Rivera's starting point for these ethical and methodological questions is expropriated property is not incidental: one place where we begin to see reckonings between long (colonial) pasts and colonial presents, where the chain of time becomes less ephemeral (though no less convoluted), is in histories of antiquities and manuscripts.[184] As both Maldonado Rivera and Annette Yoshiko Reed point out, though, in order to fully appreciate our long historical legacies, our colonial morass, we will need to perhaps first denaturalize the centrality of the usual figures, languages, and geographies that structure the study of religion in late antiquity. As the field begins to redescribe itself as "global late antiquity," Reed suggests that we must take stock of "how we are accustomed to globalizing certain Christian perspectives anyway" – the absorption of Christianity's timeline into European

---

[182] Maldonado Rivera, "Method, ethics, and historiography."

[183] Maldonado Rivera, "Method, ethics, and historiography."

[184] This is in part because the politics and ethics of antiquities collection and appropriation have been getting more attention. See the Duke University Manuscript Migration Lab, for instance, codirected by Jennifer Knust, Andrew Armacost, and William Johnson, which traces the provenance of manuscripts and considers the "ethical, legal, and political dimensions of cultural heritage as it is situated within global markets, networks, and political systems, and shaped by colonial, imperialistic, and national ideologies" (https://fhi.duke.edu/labs/manuscript-migration-lab).

modernity, for instance, or Christianity as the prototype for "religion."[185] Reed suggests here (as in her earlier coedited volume) that we "provincialize Christianity," taking a cue from Dipesh Chakrabarty's *Provincializing Europe.*

A project provincializing Christianity and interrupting linear and normativizing temporalities will need to be thoroughgoing and ongoing. I think it will also need to unfold in tandem with another colonial epistemological conundrum: how we deal with theory itself.

Conclusion: Theory and Its Uses

I want to return to Barbara Christian's "The Race for Theory," an essay about a number of things. One of those things is the way "theory" signaled a certain style and genealogy of philosophical writings and excluded Black theorizing outside of this style and genealogy including, especially, Black art and literature. Decades have passed since the publication of Christian's essay. In the intervening time, especially in the past decade, Black writers and artists (at least in certain circumstances) have more frequently appeared in or near the theory canon. The dynamics of "the race for theory" have changed.

Of course another brilliant critique implicit to Christian's essay is the way "theory" appears in the academic ecosystem, as part of the contest – the race – for what is next, what is new, what is "edgy." Theory is how to be *au courant.* This race for the trendy stands in high contrast to the dire necessity and life-giving capacity of theorizing the conditions of the world, through various means and media, when and for whom those conditions are most pressing and grim. In the former case, theory becomes currency to have, a commodity in circulation, a demonstration to make. In the latter, it is creativity and praxis, a process of reorientation to the world, and a way to sustain.[186]

What is interesting is that while the dynamics diagnosed in the first critique in "the race for theory" have changed, the dynamics diagnosed in the second critique have not. In other words, in the academic ecosystem, theories and expressions of minoritized scholars and groups often come with their own special currency – even while academic institutions continue their major terrors and minor hostilities against those same scholars and populations. In this way, the expressions and theories of minoritized people become add-ons, plus ones to white projects, and something from which historically white disciplines, institutions, and scholars benefit, or at least use to try to stay relevant. As Dan-el Padilla Peralta and Sasha-Mae Eccleston write in "Racing the Classics: Ethos

---

[185] Annette Yoshiko Reed, "Method, ethics, and historiography: Tracing a global late antiquity from and beyond Christianity," *Ancient Jew Review,* January 26, 2022.

[186] As Kevin Quashie notes in his lovely reading of Barbara Christian's essay in *Black Aliveness, Or A Poetics of Being* (Duke University Press, 2021), especially pages 133–134.

and Praxis," their devastating and thorough account of the ongoing racialized forcefield that is Classics, "The academy continues to pour resources not into a genuinely anti-racist and decolonial 21st century university, but into a commodification of color that sidesteps the hard work of institutional change."[187] Borrowing from Roderick Ferguson's book *The Reorder of Things: The University and Its Pedagogies of Minority Difference*, they elaborate: "The academy's 'adaptive hegemony,' to use Ferguson's phrasing, enables the effective containment and policing of radical change without taking an overtly oppositional stance; it can co-opt, placate, and reinvent itself without fundamentally altering how it operates or who operates in its name, and without ceding any ground in the transnational knowledge industry."[188] The piece appears in *American Journal of Philology* and Eccleston and Padilla Peralta call for a coming to grips with the dependence of philology on racial science. They do not, for instance, call for making philology Black.[189] They also call for comprehensive refiguring of goals and ways of being in the field/the academy, things like gatekeeping under the cover of "rigor," careerist individualism, and the disincentivizing of genuinely collective work.

The moderating and coopting uses of theory resonate with what Max Liboiron and Eve Tuck have described as "extractive" readings. Tuck coined the phrase "extractive readings" in a Twitter thread to describe especially the ways indigenous texts and critiques have been skimmed for leverageable concepts: reading "for discovery."[190] Liboiron recognized this tendency:

> Tuck's thread shocked me into reflexivity because, while I try to stay in good relations, I often – usually – read extractively, looking for bits I can use. I had been reading in a Resource relation ... that is unidirectional, assessing texts solely for my own goals and not approaching them as bodies of work, events, gifts, teachers, letters, or any number of other ways that would make unidirectional, extractive relations seem rude and out of place. (35)

Liboiron describes his strategies for writing less extractively and supporting his readers in reading less extractively, and many of those strategies involve giving *time and space* to concepts and their contexts of emergence.[191]

What does integrity look like within and despite the machine of academic production? For one, it requires moving away from extractive reading practices

---

187 Sasha-Mae Eccleston and Dan-el Padilla Peralta, "Racing the classics: Ethos and praxis," *American Journal of Philology*, 143 (2022), 204.

188 Eccleston and Padilla Peralta, "Racing the classics," 205.

189 Eccleston and Padilla Peralta, "Racing the classics," 210.

190 Eve Tuck, "To watch the white settlers sift through our work as they ask, 'isn't there more for me here?'" Thread, Twitter @tuckeve, October 8, 2017.

191 Max Liboiron, *Pollution Is Colonialism* (Duke University Press, 2021), 35.

and values – noticing, for instance, the way being a prodigious ("voracious") reader can also carry eerie consumptive and acquisitive subtexts. Extraction is the trained habits of academics, so I do not expect any collective de-habituation to be easy. It would be "unlearning imperialism," as Ariella Azoulay puts it.[192] Azoulay describes this unlearning work as "rehearsals with others." She writes, "Unlearning is a way of disengaging from political initiatives, concepts or modes of thinking, *including critical theory*, that are devised and promoted as progressive and unprecedented. Instead, it insists that finding precedents – or at least assuming precedents could be found – for resistance to racial and colonial crimes is not the novel work of academic discovery."[193] The drive for the novel is, in fact, a rather significant dimension of how imperialism works. As Azoulay writes further on, "The imperial movement of progress is pursued on the one hand as if along a single, straight line of advance, while on the other, it operates in a suicidal cycle where the new can hardly survive the constant and renewable threat of being declared unfit by the newest. The new is an imperial incentive."[194]

So too doing academic work with integrity requires examining the imperial-izing subtexts of collective impulses for the novel, the new, that theory often satisfies. It is unclear, though, *why* exactly theory is associated with the new and the novel, since as I have shown, theorizing (at least in this field) has meant staying for a long time with long-running, unresolved, and unresolvable ques-tions about bodies, about agency, about time, about violence, and about social lives and power. The same questions and conundrums keep appearing with variations across the history of the field. In that way, the best hope of theory as it stands is not a push for new solutions to old problems (or new solutions to new problems), or the "charting of new territory." It is its iterative returns, its penchant for thickened entanglements.

Perhaps the reason "theory" tends to represent the "new," the trendy, is to preserve by contrast a sense of traditional history, with its evidentiary loves and its reticence to conjecture, as old and stable foundation. One "brings" theory "to" historical work. That little prepositional move allows one to believe, credulously, that historical work is *something other than speculation*. It pre-serves the past as a known or at least knowable territory, a there and then that can be, must be, protected from here and now. A past unflustered by the exigencies of the present, by the tender *what if* and the anguished *why*.

---

[192] Azoulay, *Potential History*. Both Christian and Liboiron connect their reading and writing practices with ethics. These ethics are part of a more expansive set of relationships and comportments in the world. In other words, our dealings with theory are not only "in theory," they are also a practice.
[193] Azoulay, *Potential History*, 49–50. Emphasis mine.   [194] Azoulay, *Potential History*, 51.

The horizon of "theory" in this field then is not only more ethical reading practices and sincere attention to intellectual, relational, and institutional ecologies. It is the recognition that the work of history is nothing more and nothing less than the work of theorization; the work of living, one way or another, with pasts that persist.

References

Ahmed, Sara, *Cultural Politics of Emotion* (New York: Routledge, 2004).

Ahmed, Sara, *Living a Feminist Life* (Durham, NC: Duke University Press, 2017).

Ahmed, Sara, *The Promise of Happiness* (Durham, NC: Duke University Press, 2010).

Armour, Ellen T., and Susan M. St. Ville (eds.), *Bodily Citations: Religion and Judith Butler* (New York: Columbia University Press, 2006).

Azoulay, Ariella, *Potential History: Unlearning Imperialism* (London: Verso, 2019).

Baker, Cynthia M., *Rebuilding the House of Israel: Architectures of Gender in Jewish Antiquity* (Stanford, CA: Stanford University Press, 2002).

Balberg, Mira, *Purity, Body, and Self in Early Rabbinic Literature* (Berkeley: University of California Press, 2014).

Becker, Adam, and Annette Yoshiko Reed (eds.), *The Ways That Never Parted: Jews and Christians in Late Antiquity and the Early Middle Ages* (Minneapolis, MN: Fortress Press, 2007).

Belser, Julia Watts, *Rabbinic Tales of Destruction: Gender, Sex, and Disability in the Ruins of Jerusalem* (New York: Oxford University Press, 2017).

Bennett, Jane, *Vibrant Matter: A Political Ecology of Things* (Durham, NC: Duke University Press, 2010).

Berkovitz, A. J., and Mark Letteney (eds.), *Rethinking "Authority" in Late Antiquity: Authorship, Law, and Transmission in Jewish and Christian Tradition* (New York: Routledge, 2018).

Berkowitz, Beth, *Execution and Invention: Death Penalty Discourse in Early Rabbinic and Christian Culture* (New York: Oxford University Press, 2006).

Berzon, Todd, *Classifying Christians: Ethnography, Heresiology, and the Limits of Knowledge in Late Antiquity* (Berkeley: University of California Press, 2021).

Bhabha, Homi, *The Location of Culture* (New York: Routledge, 1994)

Bouchard, D. F., *Language, Counter-memory, and Practice: Selected Essays and Interviews* (Ithaca, NY: Cornell University Press, 1997).

Bourdieu, Pierre, *The Logic of Practice* (Stanford, CA: Stanford University Press, 1980).

Boustan, Ra'anan, Alex P. Jassen, and Calvin J. Roetzel (eds.), *Violence, Scripture, and Textual Practice in Early Judaism and Christianity* (Leiden: Brill, 2010).

Boustan, Raʿanan, and Joseph E. Sanzo, "Christian magicians, Jewish magical idioms, and the shared magical culture of late antiquity," *Harvard Theological Review*, 110 (2017), 217–240.

Boyarin, Daniel, *Border Lines: The Partition of Judeao-Christianity* (Philadelphia: University of Pennsylvania Press, 2006).

Boyarin, Daniel, *Dying for God: Martyrdom and the Making of Christianity and Judaism* (Stanford, CA: Stanford University Press, 1999).

Boyarin, Daniel, *A Radical Jew: Paul and the Politics of Identity* (Berkeley: University of California Press, 1997).

Boyarin, Daniel, and Elizabeth Castelli, "Foucault's 'The history of sexuality': The fourth volume or, A field left fallow for others to till," *Journal of the History of Sexuality*, 10 (2001), 357–374.

Brakke, David, "Ethiopian demons: Male sexuality, the black-skinned other, and the monastic self," *Journal of the History of Sexuality*, 10 (2011), 501–535.

Brown, Peter, *The Body and Society: Men, Women, and Sexual Renunciation in Early Christianity.* 20th anniversary ed. (New York: Columbia University Press, 2008).

Brown, Peter, *The Making of Late Antiquity* (Cambridge, MA: Harvard University Press, 1978).

Buell, Denise, *Why This New Race? Ethnic Reasoning in Early Christianity* (New York: Columbia University Press, 2005).

Burrus, Virginia, *Ancient Christian Ecopoetics: Cosmologies, Saints, Things* (Philadelphia: University of Pennsylvania Press, 2018).

Burrus, Virginia, *Begotten Not Made: Conceiving Manhood in Late Antiquity* (Stanford, CA: Stanford University Press, 2000).

Burrus, Virginia, *Chastity As Autonomy: Women in the Stories of the Apocryphal Acts* (Lewiston, NY: Edwin Mellen Press, 1987).

Burrus, Virginia, "The heretical woman as symbol in Alexander, Athanasius, Epiphanius, and Jerome," *Harvard Theological Review*, 84 (1991), 229–248.

Burrus, Virginia, "Macrina's tattoo," *Journal of Medieval and Early Modern Studies*, 33 (2003), 403–417.

Burrus, Virginia, "Mimicking virgins: Colonial ambivalence and the ancient romance," *Arethusa*, 38 (2005), 49–88.

Burrus, Virginia, *Saving Shame: Martyrs, Saints, and Other Abject Subjects* (Philadelphia: University of Pennsylvania Press, 2013).

Burrus, Virginia, *The Sex Lives of Saints: An Erotics of Ancient Hagiography* (Philadelphia: University of Pennsylvania Press, 2007).

Butler, Judith, *Bodies That Matter: On the Discursive Limits of Sex* (New York: Routledge, 1996).

Butler, Judith, *Gender Trouble: Feminism and the Subversion of Identity* (New York: Routledge, 1990).

Butler, Judith, *Undoing Gender* (New York: Routledge, 2004).

Byron, Gay L., *Symbolic Blackness and Ethnic Difference in Early Christian Literature* (New York: Routledge, 2002).

Cameron, Averil, "Redrawing the map: Early Christian territory after Foucault," *Journal of Roman Studies*, 76 (1986), 266–271.

Campbell, Timothy, and Adam Sitze (eds.), *Biopolitics: A Reader* (Durham, NC: Duke University Press, 2013).

Césaire, Suzanne, *The Great Camouflage: Writings of Dissent (1941–1945)*, ed. Daniel Mamin (Middletown, CT: Wesleyan University Press, 2012).

Chalmers, Matthew, "Past Paul's Jewishness: The Bejaminite Paul in Epiphanius of Cyrus," *Harvard Theological Review*, 115 (2022), 309–330.

Chin, Catherine Michael, "Apostles and aristocrats," in Catherine Michael Chin and Caroline T. Schroeder (eds.), *Melania: Early Christianity through the Life of One Family* (Berkeley: University of California Press, 2017), 19–33.

Chin, Catherine Michael, "Cosmos," in Catherine Michael Chin and Moulie Vidas (eds.), *Late Ancient Knowing: Explorations in Intellectual History* (Berkeley: University of California Press, 2015), 99–116.

Chin, Catherine Michael, *Grammar and Christianity in the Late Roman World* (Philadelphia: University of Pennsylvania Press, 2008).

Chin, Catherine Michael, "Marvelous things heard: On finding historical radiance," *Massachusetts Review*, 58 (2017), 478–491.

Chin, Catherine Michael, "Review of *The Tiny and the Fragmented: Miniature, Broken, or Otherwise Incomplete Objects in the Ancient World*, S. Rebecca Martin and Stephanie M. Langin-Hooper (eds.) (New York: Oxford University Press, 2018)," *Bryn Mawr Classical Review*, December 2020.

Chow, Rey, *The Age of the World Target: Self-Referentiality in War, Theory, and Comparative Work* (Durham: Duke University Press, 2006).

Chow, Rey, *A Face Drawn in Sand: Humanistic Inquiry and Foucault in the Present* (New York: Columbia University Press, 2021).

Clark, Elizabeth A., *Jerome, Chrysostom, and Friends: Essays and Translations*. 2nd ed. (Toronto: Edwin Mellen Press, 1982).

Clark, Elizabeth A., "Foucault, the fathers, and sex," *Journal of the American Academy of Religion*, 56 (1988), 619–641.

Clark, Elizabeth A., *History, Theory, Text: Historians and the Linguistic Turn* (Cambridge: Harvard University Press, 2004).

Clark, Elizabeth A., "The lady vanishes: Dilemmas of a feminist historian after the 'linguistic turn,'" *Church History*, 67 (1998), 1–31.

Clark, Elizabeth A., "The retrospective self," *Catholic Historical Review*, 101 (2015).

Clements, Niki Kasumi, "Foucault's Christianities," *Journal of the American Academy of Religion*, 89 (2021), 1–40.

Clements, Niki Kasumi, *Sites of the Ascetic Self: John Cassian and Christian Ethical Formation* (South Bend: University of Notre Dame Press, 2020).

Cobb, Stephanie, *Dying to Be Men: Gender and Language in Early Christian Martyr Texts* (New York: Columbia University Press, 2008).

Concannon, Cavan, *Assembling Early Christianity: Trade, Networks, and the Letters of Dionysios of Corinth* (Cambridge: Cambridge University Press, 2017).

Cvetkovich, Ann, *An Archive of Feelings: Trauma, Sexuality, and Lesbian Public Cultures* (Durham, NC: Duke University Press, 2007).

Cvetkovich, Ann, *Depression: A Public Feeling* (Durham, NC: Duke University Press, 2012).

Daniel-Hughes, Carly, "Adornments of empire: Feminine subjectivity and Roman colonial life in Tertullian of Carthage." Delivered at the 12th Enoch Nangeroni Meeting, "Constructions of Gender in Late Antiquity."

Daniel-Hughes, Carly, "Mary Magdalene in the fantasy echo: Reflections on the feminist historiography of early Christianity," in Taylor G. Petrey et al. (eds.), *Re-making the World: Christianity and Categories, Essays in Honor of Karen L. King* (Tübingen: Mohr Siebeck, 2019), 135–159.

Daniel-Hughes, Carly, *The Salvation of the Flesh in Tertullian of Carthage: Dressing for Resurrection* (New York: Palgrave, 2011).

Daniel-Hughes, Carly, and Maia Kotrosits, "Tertullian of Carthage and the fantasy life of power: On martyrs, Christians, and other attachments to juridical scenes," *Journal of Early Christian Studies*, 28 (2020), 1–31.

Dean, Mitchell, "Foucault must not be defended," *History and Theory*, 54 (2015), 389–403.

Deleuze, Gilles, and Félix Guattari, *Anti-Oedipus: Capitalism and Schizophrenia* (Minneapolis: University of Minnesota Press, 1983).

Deleuze, Gilles, and Félix Guattari, *A Thousand Plateaus*, trans. Brian Massumi (London: Athlone Press, 2001).

Dilts, Andrew, "From 'entrepreneur of the self' to 'care of the self': Neo-liberal governmentality and Foucault's ethics," *Foucault Studies*, 12 (2011), 130–146.

Dinkler, Michal Beth, *Literary Theory and the New Testament* (New Haven, CT: Yale University Press, 2019).

Dinkler, Michal Beth, "Pauline epistles as affective technologies: Liberating literary form and the letter to Philemon," *Biblical Interpretation*, 30 (2022), 556–577.

Dinshaw, Carolyn, *Getting Medieval: Sexualities and Communities, Pre- and Postmodern* (Durham, NC: Duke University Press, 1999).

Doerfler, Maria, *Jephthah's Daughter, Sarah's Son: The Death of Children in Late Antiquity* (Berkeley: University of California Press, 2020).

Drake, Susanna, *Slandering the Jew: Sexuality and Difference in Early Christian Texts* (Philadelphia: University of Pennsylvania, 2013).

Derrida, Jacques, *Of Grammatology* (Baltimore, MD: Johns Hopkins University Press, 1998).

Dunning, Benjamin, *Aliens and Sojourners: Self As Other in Early Christianity* (Philadelphia: University of Pennsylvania Press, 2009).

Dunning, Benjamin, *Specters of Paul: Sexual Difference in Early Christian Thought* (Philadelphia: University of Pennsylvania Press, 2011).

Eccleston, Sasha-Mae, and Dan-el Padilla Peralta, "Racing the classics: Ethos and praxis," *American Journal of Philology*, 143 (2022), 199–218.

Effros, Bonnie, *Incidental Archaeologists: French Officers and the Rediscovery of Roman North Africa* (Ithaca, NY: Cornell University Press, 2018).

Eng, David L., and Jasbir K. Puar, "Introduction in 'Left of Queer,'" *Social Text*, 145 (2020), 1–23.

Fewster, Greg, "Dying and rising with the author: Specters of Paul and the material text," in Clarssa Breu (ed.), *Biblical Exegesis without Authorial Intention? Interdisciplinary Approaches to Authorship and Meaning* (Leiden: Drill, 2019), 149–183.

Fisher, Greg, *Between Empires: Arabs, Romans, and Sasanians in Late Antiquity* (New York: Oxford University Press, 2011).

Foucault, Michel, *The History of Sexuality. Volume 1: An Introduction* (New York: Vintage Press, 1990).

Foucault, Michel, *The History of Sexuality. Volume 4: Confessions of the Flesh*, ed. Frederic Gros, trans. Robert Hurley (New York: Pantheon, 2021).

Foucault, Michel, *Language, Counter-memory, Practice* (Ithaca, NY: Cornell University Press, 1977).

Foucault, Michel, *Madness and Reason: A History of Insanity in the Age of Reason* (New York: Vintage, 1988).

Foucault, Michel, *The Order of Things: An Archaeology of the Human Sciences* (New York: Random House, 1970).

Frankfurter, David, *Christianizing Egypt: Syncretism and Local Worlds in Late Antiquity* (Princeton, NJ: Princeton University Press, 2018).

Freccero, Carla, *Queer/Early/Modern* (Durham, NC: Duke University Press, 2006).

Gallop, Jane, *The Deaths of the Author: Reading and Writing in Time* (Durham, NC: Duke University Press, 2011).

Given, J. Gregory, "Ignatius of Antioch and the historiography of early Christianity." Unpublished doctoral dissertation. Harvard University. 2019.

Gonzalez, Justo, *The Mestizo Augustine: A Theologian between Two Cultures* (Westmont, IL: Intervarsity Press, 2016).

Gossett, Reina, Eric A. Stanley, and Johanna Burton (eds.), *Trap Door: Trans Cultural Production and the Politics of Visibility* (Boston: MIT Press, 2017).

Gregg, Melissa, and Gregory J. Seigworth (eds.), *The Affect Theory Reader* (Durham, NC: Duke University Press, 2010).

Gribetz, Sarit Kattan, *Time and Difference in Rabbinic Judaism* (Princeton, NJ: Princeton University Press, 2020).

Gribetz, Sarit Kattan, "Women as readers of the Nag Hammadi codices," *Journal of Early Christian Studies*, 26 (2018), 463–494.

Guha, Ranajit, "On some aspects of the historiography of colonial India," *Subaltern Studies*, 45 (1994), 86–91.

Haines-Eitzen, Kim, *The Gendered Palimpsest: Women, Writing, and Representation in Early Christianity* (New York: Oxford University Press, 2011).

Hartman, Saidiya, "Venus in two acts," *Small Axe*, 26 (2008), 1–14.

Hartman, Saidiya, *Wayward Lives, Beautiful Experiments: Intimate Histories of Social Upheaval* (New York: W. W. Norton and Company, 2019).

Hemmings, Clare, *Why Stories Matter: The Political Grammar of Feminist Theory* (Durham, NC: Duke University Press, 2011).

Heng, Geraldine, *The Invention of Race in the European Middle Ages* (Cambridge: Cambridge University Press, 2018).

Heyes, Cressida J., *The Anaesthetics of Existence: Experience at the Edge* (Durham: Duke University Press, 2020).

Heyes, Cressida J., *Self-Transformations: Foucault, Ethics, and Normalized Bodies* (New York: Oxford University Press, 2007).

Hunt, Thomas, 'Imperial collapse and Christianization in patristic scholarship during the final decades of colonial Algeria, 1930-1962', *Journal of Early Christian Studies* 29 (2021), 261–289.

Hunt, Thomas, "The influence of French colonial humanism on the study of late antiquity: Braudel, Marrou, Brown," *International Journal of Francophone Studies*, 21 (2019), 255–278.

Hylen, Susan, *A Modest Apostle: Thecla and the History of Women in the Early Church* (New York: Oxford University Press, 2015).

Irigaray, Luce, *An Ethics of Sexual Difference*, trans. Carolyn Burke and Gillian Gill (Ithaca, NY: Cornell University Press, 1983).

Irigaray, Luce, *Speculum of the Other Woman*, trans. Gillian Gill (Ithaca, NY: Cornell University Press, 1985).

Jacobs, Andrew, *Christ Circumcised: A Study in Early Christian History and Difference* (Philadelphia: University of Pennsylvania Press, 2012).

Jacobs, Andrew, *Remains of the Jew: The Holy Land and Christian Empire in Late Antiquity* (Stanford, CA: Stanford University Press, 2003).

Jacobs, Andrew, "'Solomon's salacious song': Foucault's author function and the early Christian interpretation of the Canticum Canticorum," *Medieval Encounters*, 4 (1998), 1–23.

Jaffee, Martin S., "Rabbinic authorship as a collective enterprise," in Charlotte Elisheva Fonrobert and Martin S. Jaffee (eds.), *The Cambridge Companion to the Talmud and Rabbinic Literature* (Cambridge: Cambridge University Press, 2007), 17–37.

James, C. L. R., *The Black Jacobins: Toussaint L'Ouverture and the San Domingo Revolution* (London: Secker and Warburg, 1938).

Johnson, Aaron, *Ethnicity and Argumentation in Eusebius' Praeparatio Evangelica* (New York: Oxford University Press, 2006).

Kaldellis, Anthony, "Late antiquity dissolves," *Marginalia Review of Books*, September 18, 2015.

Keel, Terrence, *Divine Variations: How Christian Thought Became Racial Science* (Stanford, CA: Stanford University Press, 2018).

Kessler, Gwynn, *Conceiving Israel: The Fetus in Rabbinic Narratives* (Philadelphia: University of Pennsylvania Press, 2009).

King, Karen L., "Factions, diversity, multiplicity: Representing early Christian differences for the 21st century," *Method and Theory in the Study of Religion*, 23 (2011), 216–237.

King, Karen L., "'What is an author?' Ancient author function in the Apocryphon of John and the Apocalypse of John," in William Arnal et al. (eds.), *Scribal Practices and Social Structures among Jesus Adherents: Essays in Honour of John S. Kloppenborg* (London: Peeters, 2016), 15–42.

King, Karen L., *What Is Gnosticism?* (Cambridge, MA: Belknap Press, 2005).

Knight, Michael Muhammad, *Muhammad's Body: Baraka Networks and the Prophetic Assemblage* (Charlotte: University of North Carolina Press, 2020).

Knust, Jennifer, *Abandoned to Lust: Sexual Slander and Ancient Christianity* (New York: Columbia University Press, 2005).

Knust, Jennifer, "Jewish bones and Christian Bibles: The Maccabean martyrs in Christian late antiquity." Presented at the Christianity Seminar of the Westar Institute, Santa Rosa, California, 2015.

Knust, Jennifer, "Miscellany manuscripts and the Christian canonical imaginary," in Claudia Moser and Jennifer Knust (eds.), *Ritual Matters: Material Remains and Ancient Religion* (Ann Arbor: University of Michigan Press, 2017).

Knust, Jennifer, and Tommy Wasserman, *To Cast the First Stone: The Transmission of a Gospel Story* (Princeton, NJ: Princeton University Press, 2020).

Kohn, Eduardo, *How Forests Think: Toward an Anthropology beyond the Human* (Berkeley: University of California Press, 2013).

Kotrosits, Maia, "The ethnography of gender: Reconsidering gender as an object of analysis," *Studies in Late Antiquity* (forthcoming, 2023).

Kotrosits, Maia, *How Things Feel: Affect Theory, Biblical Studies, and the (Im)Personal*. Research Perspectives in Biblical Interpretation (Leiden: Brill, 2016).

Kotrosits, Maia, *The Lives of Objects: Material Culture, Experience, and the Real in the History of Early Christianity* (Chicago, IL: University of Chicago Press, 2020).

Kotrosits, Maia, "Penetration and its discontents: Greco-Roman sexuality, the Acts of Paul and Thecla, and theorizing eros without the wound," *Journal of the History of Sexuality*, 27 (2018), 343–366.

Kotrosits, Maia, *Rethinking Early Christian Identity* (Minneapolis, MN: Fortress Press, 2015).

Kraemer, Ross Shepard, *Unreliable Witnesses: Religion, Gender, and Religion in the Greco-Roman Mediterranean* (New York: Oxford University Press, 2012).

Kulisz, Abby, "Sacred friendship, holy hatred: Christian-Muslim encounters in the book in the medieval Middle East." Unpublished doctoral dissertation. Indiana University. 2022.

Larsen, Matthew D. C., *Gospels before the Book* (New York: Oxford University Press, 2018).

Latour, Bruno, *We Have Never Been Modern* (Cambridge, MA: Harvard University Press, 1993).

Le Boulluec, Alain, *La notion d'hérésie dans la littérature grecque, IIe–IIIe siècles* (Études Augustiniennes, 1985).

Liboiron, Max, *Pollution Is Colonialism* (Durham, NC: Duke University Press, 2021).

Lowe, Lisa, *The Intimacies of Four Continents* (Durham, NC: Duke University Press, 2015).

Mahmood, Saba, *The Politics of Piety: The Islamic Revival and the Feminist Subject* (Princeton, NJ: Princeton University Press, 2005).

Maldonado Rivera, David, "Method, ethics, and historiography: A late ancient Caribbean in the temporalities of empire," *Ancient Jew Review*, January 25, 2022.

Marchal, Joseph. *Appalling Bodies: Queer Figures before and after Paul's Letters* (New York: Oxford University Press, 2019).

Marrou, Henri-Irénée, 'France, ma patrie', *Le Monde*, April 5, 1956.

Marrou, Henri-Irénée, *Saint Augustin et la fin de la culture antique, avec Retractatio* (Paris: De Boccard, 1949).

Marrou, Henri-Irénée/Henri Davenson, *Fondemonts d'une culture Chretienne* (Paris: Librairie Bloud and Gay, 1934).

Martin, Dale B., and Patricia Cox Miller (eds.), *The Cultural Turn in Late Ancient Studies: Gender, Asceticism, and Historiography* (Durham, NC: Duke University Press, 2005).

Massumi, Brian, *Parables for the Virtual: Movement, Affect, Sensation* (Durham, NC: Duke University Press, 2002).

Masuzawa, Tomoko, *The Invention of World Religions: How European Universalism Was Preserved in the Language of Pluralism* (Chicago, IL: University of Chicago Press: 2005).

Mattingly, David, *Imperialism, Power, and Identity: Experiencing the Roman Empire* (Princeton, NJ: Princeton University Press, 2013).

McClintock, Anne, *Imperial Leather: Race, Gender, and Sexuality in the Colonial Contest* (New York: Routledge, 1995).

Mena, Peter Anthony, *Place and Identity in the Lives of Antony, Paul, and Mary of Egypt: Desert As Borderland* (New York: Palgrave Macmillan, 2019).

Miller, Patricia Cox, "The blazing body: Ascetic desire in Jerome's Letter to Eustochium," *Journal of Early Christian Studies*, 1(1993), 21–45.

Miller, Patricia Cox, *The Corporeal Imagination: Signifying the Holy in Late Ancient Christianity* (Philadelphia: University of Pennsylvania Press, 2009).

Miller, Patricia Cox, *The Poetry of Thought in Late Antiquity: Essays in Imagination and Religion* (New York: Routledge, 2001).

Moss, Candida, "Between the lines: Looking for contributions of enslaved literate laborers in a second-century text (P.Berol. 11632)," *Studies in Late Antiquity*, 5 (2021), 432–452.

Motia, Michael, "Bluets of late antiquity: Polychromy and Christian mysticism," *Studies in Late Antiquity*, 6 (2022), 335–369.

Muehlberger, Ellen, "On authors, fathers, and holy men," *Marginalia Review of Books*, September 20, 2015.

Muehlberger, Ellen, *Moment of Reckoning: Imagined Death and Its Consequences in Late Ancient Christianity* (New York: Oxford University Press, 2019).

Nash, Jennifer. "Black feminine enigmas, or Notes on the politics of black feminist theory," *Signs*, 45 (2020), 519–523.

Nash, Jennifer, *Black Feminism Reimagined: After Intersectionality* (Durham, NC: Duke University Press, 2018).

Nasrallah, Laura, "*Christemporos*: Christ and the market in early Christian texts, *Biblical Interpretation*," 30 (2021), 509–537.

Nasrallah, Laura, "The work of nails: Religion, Mediterranean antiquity, and contemporary black art," *Journal of the American Academy of Religion* (2022).

Nelson, Maggie, *Bluets* (New York: Wave Books, 2009).

Perkins, Judith, *The Suffering Self: Pain and Narrative Representation in the Early Christian Era* (New York: Routledge, 1995).

Petrey, Taylor, *Resurrecting Parts: Early Christians on Desire, Reproduction, and Sexual Difference* (New York: Routledge, 2016).

Porter, Sarah, "A church and its charms: Space, affect, and affiliation in late fourth-century Antioch," *Studies in Late Antiquity*, 5(2021), 641–642.

Pregill, Michael, *The Golden Calf Between Bible and Qur'an: Scripture, Polemic, and Exegesis from Late Antiquity to Islam* (New York: Oxford University Press, 2020).

Puar, Jasbir, *The Right to Maim: Debility, Capacity, Disability* (Durham, NC: Duke University Press, 2017).

Puar, Jasbir, *Terrorist Assemblages: Homonationalism in Queer Times* (Durham, NC: Duke University Press, 2007).

Quashie, Kevin, *Black Aliveness, Or A Poetics of Being* (Durham, NC: Duke University Press, 2021).

Rebillard, Éric, *Christians and Their Many Identities in Late Antiquity, North Africa, 200–450 CE* (Ithaca, NY: Cornell University Press, 2017).

Reed, Annette Yoshiko, "Method, ethics, and historiography: Tracing a global late antiquity from and beyond Christianity," *Ancient Jew Review*, January 26, 2022.

Ronis, Sara, "Imagining the other: The magical Arab in rabbinic literature," *Prooftexts*, 29 (2021), 1–28.

Said, Edward, *Culture and Imperialism* (New York: Alfred A. Knopf, 1993).

Said, Edward, *Orientalism* (New York: Pantheon, 1978).

Salamon, Gayle, *Assuming a Body: Transgender and the Rhetorics of Materiality* (New York: Columbia University Press, 2010).

Schott, Jeremy, *Christianity, Empire, and the Making of Religion in Late Antiquity* (Philadelphia: University of Pennsylvania Press, 2008).

Schroeder, Caroline T., *Children and Family in Late Antique Egyptian Monasticism* (Cambridge: Cambridge University Press, 2020).

Schroeder, Caroline T., *Monastic Bodies: Discipline and Salvation in Shenoute of Atripe* (Philadelphia: University of Pennsylvania Press, 2007).

Schroeder, Caroline T., "Women in anchoritic and semi-anchoritic monasticism in Egypt: Rethinking the landscape," *Church History*, 83 (2014), 1–17.

Scott, Joan Wallach, *The Fantasy of Feminist History* (Durham, NC: Duke University Press, 2011).

Sedgwick, Eve K., *Epistemology of the Closet* (Berkeley: University of California Press, 1990).

Sedgwick, Eve K., *Touching Feeling: Affect, Pedagogy, Performativity* (Durham, NC: Duke University Press, 2003).

Sellew, Melissa Harl, "Reading the Gospel of Thomas from here: A trans-centred hermeneutic," *Journal of Interdisciplinary Biblical Studies*, 1 (2020), 61–96.

Sharpe, Christina, *In the Wake: On Blackness and Being* (Durham, NC: Duke University Press, 2016).

Shoemaker, Stephen, *The Apocalypse of Empire: Imperial Eschatology in Late Antiquity and Early Islam* (Philadelphia: University of Pennsylvania Press, 2018).

Simpson, Audra, *Mohawk Interruptus: Political Life across Borders of Settler States* (Durham, NC: Duke University Press, 2014).

Smith, Eric, *Jewish Glass and Christian Stone: A Materialist Mapping of the "Parting of the Ways"* (New York: Routledge, 2017).

Smith, Kyle, *Constantine and the Captive Christians of Persia: Martyrdom and Religious Identity in Late Antiquity* (Berkeley: University of California Press, 2016).

Spivak, Gayatri Chakravorty, "Can the subaltern speak?" in C. Nelson and L. Grossberg (eds.), *Marxism and the Interpretation of Culture* (New York: Macmillan, 1988).

Spivak, Gayatri Chakravorty, *A Critique of Postcolonial Reason: Toward a History of the Vanishing Present* (Cambridge, MA: Harvard University Press, 1999).

Stefaniw, Blossom, *Christian Reading: Language, Ethics, and the Order of Things* (Berkeley: University of California Press, 2019).

Stefaniw, Blossom, "Feminist historiography and uses of the past," *Studies in Late Antiquity*, 4 (2020), 260–283.

Stern, Sacha, "Attribution and authorship in the Babylonian Talmud," *Journal of Jewish Studies*, 45 (1994), 28–51.

Stuelke, Patricia, *The Ruse of Repair: U.S. Neoliberal Empire and the Turn from Critique* (Durham, NC: Duke University Press, 2021).

Tuck, Eve, "To watch the white settlers fift through our work as they ask, 'Isn't there more for me here?'" Thread, Twitter @tuckeve, October 8, 2017.

Upson-Saia, Kristi, *Early Christian Dress: Gender, Virtue and Authority* (New York: Routledge, 2011).

Waller, Alexis, "Forgeries of desire: The erotics of authenticity in New Testament historiography." Unpublished doctoral dissertation. Harvard Divinity School. 2021.

Ward, Walter, *The Mirage of the Saracen: Christians and Nomads in the Sinai Peninsula in Late Antiquity* (Berkeley: University of California Press, 2014).

Weheliye, Alexander G., *Habeas Viscus: Racializing Assemblages, Biopolitcs, and Black Feminist Theories of the Human* (Durham, NC: Duke University Press, 2014).

Wiegman, Robyn, *Object Lessons* (Durham, NC: Duke University Press, 2012).

Cambridge Elements ≡

Religion in Late Antiquity

Andrew S. Jacobs
Harvard Divinity School

Andrew S. Jacobs is Senior Fellow at the Center for the Study of World Religions at Harvard Divinity School. He has taught at the University of California, Riverside, Scripps College, and Harvard Divinity School and is the author of *Remains of the Jews: The Holy Land and Christian Empire in Late Antiquity*; *Christ Circumcised: A Study in Early Christian History and Difference*; and *Epiphanius of Cyprus: A Cultural Biography of Late Antiquity*. He has co-edited *Christianity in Late Antiquity, 300–450 C.E.: A Reader and Garb of Being: Embodiment and the Pursuit of Asceticism in Late Ancient Christianity*.

About the Series
This series brings a holistic and comparative approach to religious belief and practice from 100–800 C.E. throughout the Mediterranean and Near East. Volumes will explore the key themes that characterize religion in late antiquity and will often cross traditional disciplinary lines. The series will include contributions from classical studies, Early Christianity, Judaism, and Islam, among other fields.

Cambridge Elements ☰

Religion in Late Antiquity

Elements in the Series

Theory, History, and the Study of Religion in Late Antiquity: Speculative Worlds
Maia Kotrosits

A full series listing is available at: www.cambridge.org/ELAN